Clear**Revise**

Edexcel GCSE
History 1HI0

Illustrated revision and practice

Option B4:
Early Elizabethan England, 1558–88

Published by
PG Online Limited
The Old Coach House
35 Main Road
Tolpuddle
Dorset
DT2 7EW
United Kingdom

sales@pgonline.co.uk
www.clearrevise.com
www.pgonline.co.uk
2022

PG ONLINE

PREFACE

Absolute clarity! That's the aim.

This is everything you need to ace the British depth study component of Paper 2 and beam with pride. Each topic is laid out in a beautifully illustrated format that is clear, approachable and as concise and simple as possible.

Each section of the specification is clearly indicated to help you cross-reference your revision. The checklist on the contents pages will help you keep track of what you have already worked through and what's left before the big day.

We have included worked exam-style questions with answers. There is also a set of exam-style questions at the end of each section for you to practise writing answers. You can check your answers against those given at the end of the book.

LEVELS OF LEARNING

Based on the degree to which you are able to truly understand a new topic, we recommend that you work in stages. Start by reading a short explanation of something, then try and recall what you've just read. This will have limited effect if you stop there but it aids the next stage. Question everything. Write down your own summary and then complete and mark a related exam-style question. Cover up the answers if necessary but learn from them once you've seen them. Lastly, teach someone else. Explain the topic in a way that they can understand. Have a go at the different practice questions – they offer an insight into how and where marks are awarded.

ACKNOWLEDGEMENTS

The questions in the ClearRevise textbook are the sole responsibility of the authors and have neither been provided nor approved by the examination board.

Every effort has been made to trace and acknowledge ownership of copyright. The publishers will be happy to make any future amendments with copyright owners that it has not been possible to contact. The publisher would like to thank the following companies and individuals who granted permission for the use of their images in this textbook.

Design and artwork: Jessica Webb / PG Online Ltd
Graphics / images: © Shutterstock
Images on pages 3, 5, 12, 18, 20, 31, 36, 41, 54 © Alamy
Golden Hind © cowardlion / Shutterstock
The Globe Theatre © Nick Brundle Photography / Shutterstock
Jesus College, Oxford © Tania Volosianko / Shutterstock.com
Pope Pius V © Walters Art Museum

First edition 2022   10 9 8 7 6 5 4 3 2 1
A catalogue entry for this book is available from the British Library
ISBN: 978-1-910523-43-8
Contributor: James Maroney
Copyright © PG Online 2022
All rights reserved

Printed on FSC certified paper by Bell and Bain Ltd, Glasgow, UK.

THE SCIENCE OF REVISION

Illustrations and words

Research has shown that revising with words and pictures doubles the quality of responses by students.[1] This is known as 'dual-coding' because it provides two ways of fetching the information from our brain. The improvement in responses is particularly apparent in students when they are asked to apply their knowledge to different problems. Recall, application and judgement are all specifically and carefully assessed in public examination questions.

Retrieval of information

Retrieval practice encourages students to come up with answers to questions.[2] The closer the question is to one you might see in a real examination, the better. Also, the closer the environment in which a student revises is to the 'examination environment', the better. Students who had a test 2–7 days away did 30% better using retrieval practice than students who simply read, or repeatedly reread material. Students who were expected to teach the content to someone else after their revision period did better still.[3] What was found to be most interesting in other studies is that students using retrieval methods and testing for revision were also more resilient to the introduction of stress.[4]

Ebbinghaus' forgetting curve and spaced learning

Ebbinghaus' 140-year-old study examined the rate at which we forget things over time. The findings still hold true. However, the act of forgetting facts and techniques and relearning them is what cements them into the brain.[5] Spacing out revision is more effective than cramming – we know that, but students should also know that the space between revisiting material should vary depending on how far away the examination is. A cyclical approach is required. An examination 12 months away necessitates revisiting covered material about once a month. A test in 30 days should have topics revisited every 3 days – intervals of roughly a tenth of the time available.[6]

Summary

Students: the more tests and past questions you do, in an environment as close to examination conditions as possible, the better you are likely to perform on the day. If you prefer to listen to music while you revise, tunes without lyrics will be far less detrimental to your memory and retention. Silence is most effective.[5] If you choose to study with friends, choose carefully – effort is contagious.[7]

1. Mayer, R. E., & Anderson, R. B. (1991). Animations need narrations: An experimental test of dual-coding hypothesis. *Journal of Education Psychology*, (83)4, 484–490.

2. Roediger III, H. L., & Karpicke, J.D. (2006). Test-enhanced learning: Taking memory tests improves long-term retention. *Psychological Science*, 17(3), 249–255.

3. Nestojko, J., Bui, D., Kornell, N. & Bjork, E. (2014). Expecting to teach enhances learning and organisation of knowledge in free recall of text passages. *Memory and Cognition*, 42(7), 1038–1048.

4. Smith, A. M., Floerke, V. A., & Thomas, A. K. (2016) Retrieval practice protects memory against acute stress. *Science*, 354(6315), 1046–1048.

5. Perham, N., & Currie, H. (2014). Does listening to preferred music improve comprehension performance? *Applied Cognitive Psychology*, 28(2), 279–284.

6. Cepeda, N. J., Vul, E., Rohrer, D., Wixted, J. T. & Pashler, H. (2008). Spacing effects in learning a temporal ridgeline of optimal retention. *Psychological Science*, 19(11), 1095–1102.

7. Busch, B. & Watson, E. (2019), *The Science of Learning*, 1st ed. Routledge.

CONTENTS

Option B4 Early Elizabethan England, 1558–88

Key topic 1   Queen, government and religion, 1558–69

Key topic 2   Challenges to Elizabeth at home and abroad, 1569–88

MARK ALLOCATIONS

Green mark allocations[1] on answers to 4-mark questions throughout this guide help to indicate where marks are gained within the answers. A bracketed '1' e.g. [1] = one valid point worthy of a mark. There are often many more points to make than there are marks available so you have more opportunities to max out your answers than you may think.

Higher mark questions require extended responses. These answers should be marked as a whole in accordance with the levels of response guidance on **page 61**.

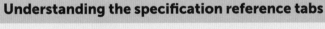

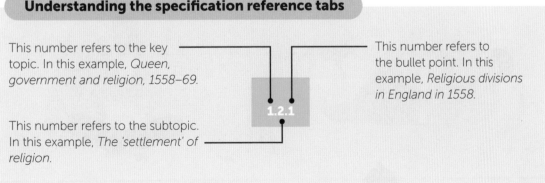

Understanding the specification reference tabs

This number refers to the key topic. In this example, *Queen, government and religion, 1558–69.*

This number refers to the bullet point. In this example, *Religious divisions in England in 1558.*

1.2.1

This number refers to the subtopic. In this example, *The 'settlement' of religion.*

THE EXAM

Paper 2 is split across two booklets. Booklet P is the Period Study and Booklet B is the British Depth Study. This revision guide covers Booklet B4. The questions follow the same format every year, so make sure you're familiar with them before the big day.

Q1 (a)   'Describe two features of...'

This question tests your **knowledge** of key features of the period. It's worth four marks and you will be awarded one mark for each feature identified (maximum of two features) and one mark for supporting information for each feature (maximum of two marks). Since it's only worth four marks, don't spend too long on this question.

Q1 (b)   'Explain why...'

This question tests your understanding of **causation** (**why** something happened). You need to use your own knowledge, but there will be two stimulus points to help you. To get top marks, you need to include information that goes beyond these stimulus points. This question is worth 12 marks, so make sure your answer includes sufficient detail.

Q1 (c)   'How far do you agree...'

For Q1 (c), you'll have the choice of two questions but you only need to answer one. Both questions will give a statement, and you need to say how far you agree with it. This question is worth 16 marks and it tests your knowledge of **cause**, **consequence**, **change**, **continuity**, **significance**, **similarity** and **difference**. You'll be given two stimulus points, but you also need to include your own knowledge to secure the top marks. Your answer needs to reach a judgement and it must be justified with supporting evidence.

TOPICS FOR PAPER 2
BRITISH DEPTH STUDY

Option B4:
Early Elizabethan England, 1558–88

Information about Paper 2

Written exam: 1 hour 45 minutes (This includes the Period study)
64 marks (32 marks for each of the British Depth study and the Period study)
40% of the qualification grade (20% for each of the British Depth study and the Period study)

Specification coverage

Key topic 1: Queen, government and religion, 1558–69

Key topic 2: Challenges to Elizabeth at home and abroad, 1569–88

Key topic 3: Elizabethan society in the Age of Exploration, 1558–88

Questions

Answer questions 1(a), 1(b) and either 1(c)(i) or 1(c)(ii)

ELIZABETHAN ENGLAND IN 1558: SOCIETY AND GOVERNMENT

As the Queen of England, Elizabeth was the most powerful person in the country. Everyone was expected to obey her.

Elizabeth's role in government

Elizabeth had the power to:

declare war and make peace (foreign affairs).

rule on some court cases.

distribute land, titles, and jobs to keep people loyal (**patronage**).

call and dismiss Parliament.

Structure of national government

Those closest to Elizabeth held the most influence.

Court

Elizabeth's court was made up of her closest servants, friends and advisors. Admittance was by invitation only. The court's role was to guide and entertain Elizabeth, as well as to display her wealth and power.

Privy Council

The Privy (private) Council was made up of approximately 20 crown-appointed nobles. These were senior and trusted figures who advised Elizabeth and administered and enforced government in areas of religion, economy, and defence. They oversaw local government through **Justices of the Peace** (JPs) (see next page) and monitored Parliament.

Parliament

Parliament was made up of the **House of Lords** (bishops and nobles) and an 'elected' **House of Commons** (gentry). Parliament advised the monarch, passed laws (called **Acts of Parliament**) and could grant extraordinary taxation, but it was relatively weak and was only called 13 times under Elizabeth.

Structure of local government

Lord-Lieutenants

Crown-appointed nobles, one for each county, who raised and maintained local armies, enforced local government, and supervised the JPs. They were often part of the Privy Council.

Justices of the Peace (JPs)

Large landowners who volunteered to enforce crown policy and maintain law and order through county courts. There were about 40 JPs in each county.

Change   Securing loyalty

Elizabeth kept noble families loyal using **patronage**. Patronage rewarded people by granting them titles and money. This tied noble families to Elizabeth and reduced the influence of other, less loyal, families.

Elizabeth trusted few people, but she did rely on **William Cecil** (her closest advisor and Secretary of State until 1572), **Robert Dudley**, **Nicholas Bacon** and, later, **Francis Walsingham**.

William Cecil presiding over a council.

Describe **two** features of government in early Elizabethan England. [4]

> *Parliament had limited influence as the Privy Council was more important.*[1] *Elizabeth had the power to call and dismiss Parliament but only called it 13 times in her reign.*[1]
>
> *Lord-Lieutenants helped to enforce local government.*[1] *They were appointed by Elizabeth and helped to raise and maintain local armies.*[1]

Elizabethan society

Elizabethan **hierarchy** was fixed. Everyone knew their place in society.

The monarch was at the top of the hierarchy, second to God in the Great Chain of Being. People owed obedience to those above them and had a duty of care to those below them. Men were the head of the household and had authority over their wives and children. Workplace relations followed this structure too and employers expected obedience from their employees.

In towns and cities

Social position was based on wealth and occupation.

- **Merchants** were often wealthy traders who owned substantial property.
- **Professionals** worked in a respected job, e.g., the **clergy** (church), lawyers or doctors.
- **Craftsmen** had learnt a skill or trade and were further structured depending on whether they owned a business or not. Skilled crafts included carpentry and tailoring.
- **Unskilled labourers** and the **unemployed** were the lowest rung on the urban hierarchy.

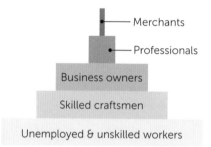

In the countryside

90% of the population lived in the countryside, and social position was related to land.

- Members of the **nobility** (lords, earls and dukes) were often the largest landowners.
- The **gentry** owned smaller estates than nobles, but more than **yeomen** who owned much smaller sized estates and land.
- Beneath these landowners were **tenant farmers** who rented land from the gentry and yeomen.
- The **labouring poor** and **landless** had to work to support their families.
- At the very bottom were **vagrants** (the homeless). There was an increase in poverty during Elizabeth's reign (see **page 48**), so vagrancy was on the rise.

THE VIRGIN QUEEN

When Elizabeth came to the throne in 1558, some people believed she shouldn't rule England.

Challenges faced by Elizabeth

Her legitimacy: There were doubts about whether Elizabeth's parents (Henry VIII and Anne Boleyn) had been legally married when Elizabeth was born.

Anne Boleyn (1501–1536)

Significance   Legitimacy

The Pope denied **Henry VIII**'s request to divorce his first wife, Catherine of Aragon. In response, Henry began the **English Reformation**, and created the **Church of England**, with himself as its head. He then granted himself a divorce and married **Anne Boleyn**. Anne gave birth to Elizabeth in 1533 but Anne was unable to give Henry a male heir. Henry had Anne executed in 1536 and declared Elizabeth **illegitimate** after her mother's death, although he later reversed this decision.

Catholics believe that the Pope is the head of the Church, so for many Catholics, Henry's divorce and remarriage was unlawful, and they refused to accept that Elizabeth was legitimate.

Her gender: A female monarch ruling alone contradicted society's beliefs that men were superior to women. Many felt Elizabeth lacked the skills and intelligence to hold power on her own.

Her predecessor: Mary I (Elizabeth's half-sister) had ruled before Elizabeth and had left the country in debt. During her reign, England had suffered poor harvests and religious divisions. This didn't bode well for another female monarch.

Her youth: Elizabeth was only 25 when she became queen. She needed the Privy Council's advice and the support of Parliament.

Elizabeth was third in line for the throne, so no-one expected her to rule. She had a difficult childhood and wasn't really prepared to rule England.

Mary Tudor, also known as Mary I (1516–1558)

Her reluctance to marry: Tudor women were expected to marry young and have children. Elizabeth was unmarried and the last of the **Tudor dynasty** (her family line), which meant there would be no obvious successor after her death. The Privy Council worried that competition for the throne when Elizabeth died could start a **civil war** (a war between different members of the same country). However, staying unmarried meant that Elizabeth could avoid being overruled by a husband.

Significance   **Marriage**

As well as providing an heir, marriage could be useful for diplomatic or political reasons by creating a union between two countries. However, choosing the 'wrong' husband could also cause problems. Whoever she chose (Catholic, Protestant or someone from overseas) would have attracted criticism, and even choosing an English husband could have caused resentment from those who weren't chosen. She never married, so Elizabeth is known as the **Virgin Queen**.

1. Explain why Elizabeth's advisors wanted her to marry when she became queen.

   You **may** use the following in your answer:
   • Elizabeth's legitimacy
   • Elizabeth's gender

   You **must** also use information of your own.   [12]

   Your answer may include:

   Legitimacy:
   • *Doubts over the legality of Henry VIII's marriage to Anne Boleyn (especially amongst Catholics) and Henry VIII's declaration of Elizabeth's illegitimacy meant some people thought she wasn't the rightful queen. Marrying and producing an heir would make her position more stable.*

   Gender:
   • *Tudor society expected women to marry and have children, so it was unusual for Elizabeth to be unmarried. Society also believed that women were socially inferior to men, and that Elizabeth shouldn't rule without a man. Women were thought to be less powerful and intelligent. Having a husband would strengthen her position.*

   Other relevant points:
   • *Without an heir, there was no clear successor which risked civil war after Elizabeth's death.*
   • *Marriage could be used for diplomatic and political reasons to secure an ally abroad.*
   • *Elizabeth was young when she came to the throne, so an older husband could help her rule.*

   This question should be marked in accordance with the levels-based mark scheme on page 61.

Make sure your answer to this question is in paragraphs and full sentences. Bullet points have been used in this example answer to suggest some information you could include. To get top marks, you need to include information other than the bullet points in the question.

Elizabeth's character

Support from the Privy Council (and the rest of the nation) partly depended on how convincing Elizabeth could be as a ruler. Elizabeth's **character** both helped and hindered her:

Her strengths	Her weaknesses
Highly intelligent: She spoke five languages.	**Indecisive and cautious**: She kept Mary, Queen of Scots imprisoned for years because she didn't want to execute her (see **pages 22-23**).
Charismatic and confident: She delivered inspiring speeches, such as the speech to troops waiting to defend England from the Spanish Armada.	**Angered easily**: She had a fiery temper and was prone to bouts of anger.
Resilient: She had been imprisoned in the Tower of London before she became queen.	
Politically wise: She cleverly dealt with the issue of being unmarried by saying she was married to her country.	

Change   Propaganda

Elizabeth used **propaganda** to increase support for her reign. She used portraits and court plays to portray herself as strong and pure. Elizabeth's royal progress (a trip around the country) also boosted her popularity.

Elizabeth

2. Describe **two** features of Elizabeth's character.   [4]

Elizabeth was politically wise.[1] She used propaganda, such as a royal progress, to boost her popularity with her subjects. [1]

Elizabeth was cautious.[1] She took a long time to make decisions and only trusted a limited number of advisors, such as William Cecil.[1]

CHALLENGES AT HOME AND ABROAD

Elizabeth faced several challenges when she became queen.

Threats to Elizabeth's rule in 1558

Religious division: Mary I had violently persecuted Protestants during her reign, and there were tensions between Catholics and Protestants (see **pages 10-11**).

External threats: Elizabeth's Protestant faith, lack of an heir and doubts about her legitimacy meant her position as queen wasn't secure. This could be exploited by foreign powers looking to invade England.

Poverty: The country was recovering from poor harvests (see **page 48**) and taxation caused by Mary I's wars.

Debts: The crown was £300,000 in debt. This was more than it earnt annually (see **page 9**).

The French threat

France posed the biggest threat at the start of Elizabeth's reign.

Religion

Elizabeth was Protestant, but France was Catholic. Some feared that France might try to overthrow a weak Protestant queen with support from English Catholics.

History

France was England's oldest enemy. The two countries had been periodically at war for centuries, and when Elizabeth came to the throne, she inherited a war that had been started by Mary I. Elizabeth was quick to end this war in 1559, especially because there

were French troops in Scotland and she felt vulnerable to an invasion from the north.

France had an allegiance with Scotland (the **Auld Alliance**) which dated back centuries. When Mary, Queen of Scots returned to Scotland from France in 1561, this strengthened the ties between the two countries.

Succession

Mary, Queen of Scots (Elizabeth's second cousin) married **Francis II**, King of France in 1559. When Mary I died, Mary, Queen of Scots declared herself the rightful, Catholic queen of England. Mary had a strong claim to the throne and could gather support from Scottish, English and French Catholics.

Don't get confused between Mary I and Mary, Queen of Scots. Mary I (also known as 'Bloody Mary') was Elizabeth's half-sister. Mary, Queen of Scots was Elizabeth's cousin.

The financial threat

Elizabeth needed money for patronage and to fund wars, but the Crown was in enormous amounts of debt and raising taxes would be unpopular.

Reasons for debt

Mary I had sold crown lands to finance wars. Although this provided money in the short term, it led to less annual rental income during Elizabeth's reign. Mary I had also borrowed money from abroad with high levels of interest.

The English currency had been **debased** (the gold and silver content had been steadily reduced) for years prior to 1558. This meant foreign merchants were reluctant to accept English money which damaged English trade.

Sources of income

Elizabeth received taxes from her subjects, but she needed Parliament to approve extra taxes. Raising taxes would be unpopular and could lead to unrest. England was also suffering from **inflation** (where prices rose, but wages didn't) which meant the poor were already struggling.

Explain why France posed a threat to Elizabeth's rule at the start of her reign.

You **may** use the following in your answer:

- Elizabeth's religion
- Mary, Queen of Scots

You **must** also use information of your own. [12]

Your answer may include:

Elizabeth's religion:

- *Elizabeth was a Protestant and France was a Catholic country. France could use Elizabeth's religion as an excuse to invade England.*
- *France could also use Catholic supporters in England to help overthrow Elizabeth.*

Mary Queen of Scots:

- *Mary, Queen of Scots had declared herself the rightful queen of England after Mary I died. Mary, Queen of Scots was married to the King of France, Francis II. France and Scotland had an alliance, and Mary, Queen of Scots' links to both France and Scotland strengthened this allegiance. If Mary invaded England with the support of France and Scotland, this could be very dangerous for Elizabeth.*

Other information:

- *England and France had been enemies for centuries, and they had been at war many times before. England was in a lot of debt, and couldn't afford a war with France, so this made France a real threat.*
- *When Elizabeth came to the throne, she inherited a war with France. This made Elizabeth vulnerable as France had troops stationed in Scotland, and there was the potential that France could invade from the north.*

This question should be marked in accordance with the levels-based mark scheme on page 61.

RELIGIOUS DIVISIONS IN ENGLAND IN 1558

Following Henry VIII's **Reformation** (see **page 5**), Protestants immigrated to England to escape persecution in Europe.

Different religious groups were more concentrated in certain parts of England.

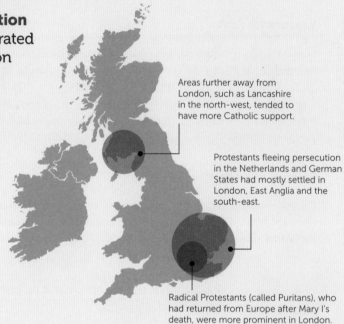

Areas further away from London, such as Lancashire in the north-west, tended to have more Catholic support.

Protestants fleeing persecution in the Netherlands and German States had mostly settled in London, East Anglia and the south-east.

Radical Protestants (called Puritans), who had returned from Europe after Mary I's death, were more prominent in London.

Religious differences

Catholicism, Protestantism and Puritanism are all forms of Christianity, but there are some significant differences in what each group believe.

Catholic beliefs

- The **Pope** was the head of the Catholic Church.
- The Church had different ecclesiastical positions, e.g., archbishops, cardinals, bishops and priests.
- Catholics believed in **transubstantiation** (the wine and bread used in communion became the blood and body of Christ).
- Church acted as the link between God and the people.
- Services were in Latin.
- Churches were very decorative, and priests wore embellished **vestments** (robes).
- Priests had to be **celibate** (unmarried).
- Catholics believed in **seven sacraments** (religious ceremonies): baptism, confirmation, Eucharist, reconciliation, anointing of the sick, matrimony and holy orders.

Pope Pius V (1504–1572), who later excommunicated Elizabeth

Protestant beliefs

- There shouldn't be a Pope.
- There shouldn't be ecclesiastical positions.
- Protestants did not believe in transubstantiation.
- The Bible acted as the link between God and the people.
- Services should be in English.
- Churches should be simple, and priests should wear plain vestments.
- Priests were allowed to marry.
- Only two sacraments were accepted, baptism and Eucharist.

Puritan beliefs

- There shouldn't be a Pope.
- There shouldn't be ecclesiastical positions because everyone is equal in the eyes of God.
- Puritans did not believe in transubstantiation.
- The Bible acted as the link between God and the people.
- Services should be in English.
- Churches should be plain white, and priests shouldn't wear vestments.
- Only two sacraments were accepted, baptism and Eucharist.

Describe **two** features of the Puritan religion in early Elizabethan England. [4]

The Bible should be someone's link to God, not church.[1] Therefore, the Bible should be in English so that everyone could understand it.[1]

Puritans thought everyone should be equal in God's eyes[1] so they didn't believe in the Pope as the head of the Church or that there should be ecclesiastical positions.[1]

ELIZABETH'S RELIGIOUS SETTLEMENT (1559)

Resolving England's religious conflict was vital at the start of Elizabeth's reign.

Religious challenges in 1558

The country was split between Catholic areas, Protestant areas and an increasing and vocal Puritan population.

Mary I's attacks on Protestantism (she had burned Protestants at the stake) had angered Protestants.

Catholic rulers in Spain, France and Scotland could invade, so Elizabeth needed to secure the loyalty of English Catholics.

Many Catholics thought Elizabeth was illegitimate.

Aims of Elizabeth's religious settlement

- Elizabeth was Protestant, and she wanted to protect and secure her faith.

- England had been a Protestant country under Edward VI and then reverted to Catholicism under Mary I. Elizabeth wanted to end religious upheaval by creating a stable and lasting settlement.

- She needed to create a form of Protestantism that would either be acceptable to the majority of Catholics or would allow them to carry on practising their own faith.

- Elizabeth wanted to use the settlement to secure her own position as monarch.

A coronation portrait of Elizabeth

The religious settlement

Elizabeth worked with the Privy Council to create the **religious settlement**. This resulted in two acts: **The Act of Supremacy** and the **Act of Uniformity**.

The Act of Uniformity 1559

The Act of Uniformity made church attendance compulsory, specified the internal appearance of churches (replacing the altar with a communion table) and banned Catholic mass. It also established a common wording for services in all churches, through the new **Book of Common Prayer**.

Deliberately unclear in some areas, the wording of the Book of Common Prayer allowed both Catholics and Protestants to interpret elements such as communion in a way they were comfortable with.

1. Describe **two** features of the 1559 religious settlement. [4]

The Act of Supremacy made Elizabeth the Supreme Governor of the Church.[1] The Oath of Supremacy meant clergy had to swear loyalty to the Queen or face punishment.[1]

The Act of Uniformity introduced the Book of Common Prayer which established the wording for church services.[1] Some wording in the Book of Common Prayer was deliberately ambiguous which allowed Catholics and Protestants to interpret it in a way they were happy with.[1]

The Act of Supremacy, 1559

The Act of Supremacy made Elizabeth **Supreme Governor** of the Church of England, rather than **Supreme Head**. This satisfied those people who felt a woman couldn't be head of the Church but effectively restored the monarch over the Pope.

All church members had to swear an oath to Elizabeth (the **Oath of Supremacy**) and could be arrested if they didn't.

The **Ecclesiastical High Commission** was established to maintain church discipline and enforce Elizabeth's settlement, punishing anyone who was disloyal.

Royal Injunctions, 1559

Royal Injunctions were issued by William Cecil on behalf of the queen to enforce the Acts of Supremacy and Uniformity. They decreed:

- all preachers needed a licence.
- fines would be issued for not attending church.
- a copy of the Bible in English would be given to each parish.
- priests were to wear special vestments for services.
- 'fake' miracles were outlawed, as were pilgrimages.
- all clergy would teach the supremacy of Elizabeth.

2. "Religious division was the biggest threat faced by Elizabeth when she first became queen."

How far do you agree? Explain your answer.

You **may** use the following in your answer:

- foreign threats
- England's financial state

You **must** also use information of your own. [16]

Your answer may include:

Agree
Religious threats:

- *There were religious divisions between Protestants and Catholics, and these divisions had been worsened by Mary I's persecution of Protestants. Religious tensions could cause unrest.*
- *Elizabeth wanted to secure her Protestant faith, but forcing Protestantism on Catholics could cause rebellions, especially in Catholic strongholds in the north.*
- *Spain and France were both Catholic countries and they could use Elizabeth's Protestantism as an excuse to invade.*

Disagree
Foreign threats:

- *France and England were old enemies who had been periodically at war for centuries. Elizabeth inherited a war from Mary I which left her vulnerable to invasion.*
- *The close ties between France and Scotland (the Auld Alliance) were strengthened when Mary, Queen of Scots returned to Scotland in 1561. Mary, Queen of Scots had a strong claim to the English throne, which threatened Elizabeth's position.*

England's financial state:

- *Elizabeth needed money for patronage and in case another country declared war, but England was £300,000 in debt.*
- *Mary had sold crown lands which reduced rental income, and the currency had been steadily debased which caused foreign trade to suffer.*
- *Bad harvests and taxation during Mary's reign meant that the population was poor. Further taxation would be unpopular and worsen poverty. Poverty could lead to domestic unrest.*

Other threats:

- *Many thought Elizabeth was unsuitable to rule England because she was female, and others thought Elizabeth was illegitimate and wasn't the rightful queen of England. This weakened Elizabeth's position as Queen.*

This question should be marked in accordance with the levels-based mark scheme on page 62.

To get top marks, you must refer to the question and make a judgement on the statement, having outlined the different sides of the argument.

Make sure your answer to this question is in paragraphs and full sentences. Bullet points have been used in this example answer to suggest some information you could include. To get top marks, you need to include information other than the bullet points in the question.

THE CHURCH OF ENGLAND AND ITS ROLE IN SOCIETY

Religion was very important during the Elizabethan period, so the Church of England was central to the lives of people across the country.

The Church in everyday life

Priests were important and trusted members of the local community who oversaw significant life events such as baptisms, communions, weddings and funerals. The church helped in times of hardship by offering charity and guidance, especially in towns where poverty and illness were more concentrated. Churches also organised religious festivals, such as Easter, which were important for bringing local people together. Priests were often among the most educated members of the community, so they were respected by their congregation.

As part of visitations (see the box overleaf) bishops would also carry out inspections of other professions, such as teachers, midwives, and surgeons, which meant they oversaw, and were involved with, much of the community.

The Church and the law

Church courts dealt with moral matters as well as internal church matters. For example, church courts could certify if a couple could legally marry, as well as resolve issues with inheritance and wills. Church courts also ruled on other legal issues, such as sexual offences, bigamy (marrying more than one person) or slander.

The Church and royal authority

The clergy were central to society, so they could ensure support for both the religious settlement and Elizabeth's rule. Following the Royal Injunctions, all priests needed a government license to preach. This meant if a priest objected to Elizabeth, she could deny him the right to preach. Bishops carried out **visitations** every 3–4 years, inspecting the clergy and their churches to ensure rules were being followed and services were being carried out as specified.

Significance	Visitations

The first visitations were carried out in 1559, and about 400 clergy were dismissed for not following the religious settlement. This resulted in a lot of vacant church positions which weren't easy to fill. Although Elizabeth wanted to control the worst examples of non-conformity to the settlement, she also realised that she needed to be more lenient, and she requested that visitations should not pry too much into people's behaviour.

During church services, the clergy would say prayers of obedience and thanks to Elizabeth, which reminded parishioners of their duty and loyalty to her.

1. Describe **two** features of the Church's role in society. [4]

   The Church oversaw important life events, such as baptisms, marriages, and funerals.[1] This made it a trusted and central part of the community.[1]

   Following the Royal Injunctions, clergy needed a government-issued licence to preach.[1] This ensured the loyalty of the clergy and meant that they could be trusted to support the Queen and uphold her authority in society.[1]

2. Explain why Elizabeth felt a religious settlement was necessary in 1559.

   You **may** use the following in your answer:

   - Elizabeth's religion
   - religious divisions in England

   You **must** also use information of your own. [12]

Your answer may include:

Elizabeth's religion:

- *Elizabeth was a Protestant and she wanted to use the religious settlement to make England a Protestant country and to protect and secure her faith.*
- *Elizabeth's religious settlement aimed to establish Protestantism in a way that would be broadly acceptable to Catholics, Protestants and Puritans.*

Religious divisions in England:

- *England was religiously divided with a concentration of Catholic nobles in the north, and Protestants and Puritans in the south. During Mary I's reign, Protestants had been violently persecuted, and Elizabeth did not want religious divisions to cause instability to her reign.*
- *Elizabeth needed to find a religious compromise to satisfy Catholics while ensuring loyalty from Protestants and Puritans who were keen to see progress.*

Other information:

- *Elizabeth's position in 1558–9 was precarious, with doubts over her legitimacy, especially amongst Catholics. Elizabeth wanted to establish her position as a Protestant monarch but needed to keep Catholics on-side to prevent them from plotting against her and replacing her with a Catholic monarch.*
- *Elizabeth needed to appease Catholics at home to prevent France and Spain from stirring up unrest amongst English Catholics.*
- *She wanted to secure her position as monarch and used the Oath of Supremacy and government-issued licences to ensure loyalty from the clergy. Loyal clergy helped to maintain the support of the public.*

This question should be marked in accordance with the levels-based mark scheme on page 61.

Make sure your answer to this question is in paragraphs and full sentences. Bullet points have been used in this example answer to suggest some information you could include. To get top marks, you need to include information other than the bullet points in the question.

THE PURITAN CHALLENGE

Puritans hoped Elizabeth's religious settlement signalled the start of a stronger move towards Protestantism. When this didn't happen, Puritan clergy led acts of opposition.

Crucifixes

The religious settlement insisted that a **crucifix** should be placed in each church. This was acceptable to Catholics, as crucifixes were an important symbol, and it wasn't too controversial to Protestants because the cross was an established Christian image. However, Puritans opposed crucifixes. They believed that they were idols, and **idolatry** (worshipping an idol as if it were God) was considered Catholic. Puritan clergy demanded the removal of crucifixes and threatened to resign if they weren't removed.

Although Elizabeth opposed their demands, she didn't have enough clergy to replace those who objected. As a result, she chose not to enforce it, and allowed crucifixes to be removed where the clergy opposed them.

The Vestment Controversy

The Royal Injunctions (see **page 13**) attempted to enforce uniformity of vestments across the Church. However, Puritans believed that priests were equal to their congregation and shouldn't wear vestments at all. The Archbishop of Canterbury, Matthew Parker, issued guidelines on vestments as part of his **Book of Advertisements** in 1566, which insisted on the established clothing. Parker also ordered clergy to attend an exhibit in London demonstrating the correct vestments. 37 priests who refused to attend were ironically de-frocked (stripped of their right to preach).

Although many Puritans opposed wearing vestments, the majority did give in and accepted Elizabeth's rules.

Significance   The Puritan response

Initially, the religious settlement seemed to be accepted by most Puritans, but it eventually met with more resistance. Although the rows over crucifixes and vestments showed there was Puritan opposition to the settlement, it never led to significant attempts to depose Elizabeth.

Describe **two** features of Puritan resistance to the 1559 religious settlement.   [4]

Some Puritan clergy opposed displaying crucifixes in churches because they thought it was idolatry.[1] Elizabeth decided not to enforce the placement of crucifixes in Puritan churches because she didn't have enough clergy to replace those who objected.[1]

Puritans opposed priests wearing vestments, believing that they shouldn't dress differently to their congregation.[1] Archbishop Matthew Parker de-frocked 37 priests who refused to wear the approved vestments.[1]

THE CATHOLIC CHALLENGE

Elizabeth wanted her religious settlement to satisfy English Catholics despite her own Protestant faith.

The impact of the religious settlement at home

With the public

Most of England's population accepted the settlement and attended church regardless of their faith. The settlement deliberately allowed interpretation and kept elements of the appearance of churches from earlier eras, so people were fairly tolerant. Elizabeth did not want to persecute people who opposed the settlement. She hoped that a gradual change would lead to a more stable Protestant nation over time.

In 1566, the Pope instructed Catholics in England to oppose the settlement by boycotting church services. Although non-attendance should have been punishable by fines, these fines weren't always enforced. It was easier for Elizabeth to overlook small infringements than create potential **martyrs** (someone who suffers for their faith).

With the clergy

There was more resistance to the settlement amongst the clergy. Around 8,000 clergy from roughly 10,000 parishes swore the oath to Elizabeth under the Act of Supremacy. Amongst the bishops, there was even more opposition. Only one bishop swore the oath to Elizabeth, so the queen was forced to replace the others with Protestant bishops. However, this was not sustainable, and meant Elizabeth needed to keep the Protestant bishops loyal throughout her reign.

With the nobility

Up to a third of the English nobility, many in the north, were **recusants** (people who practised Catholicism in secret). The northern nobles were a potential threat to the security of her reign, but Elizabeth turned a blind eye. With the nobility, it was a lack of enforcement that had an impact, rather than the settlement itself.

The Revolt of the Northern Earls (see **pages 26-28**) was a plot to overthrow Elizabeth by the Catholic nobility. This suggests that there was considerable opposition to the settlement among some nobles. However, religion wasn't the only motive for the rebellion. The nobles were also angry at a loss of power and money during Elizabeth's reign.

Change   Elizabeth's attitude

Although Elizabeth was initially tolerant of recusants, her attitude hardened after several plots against her (see **pages 29-31**) and an increase in foreign priests coming to England (see **page 20**). In 1581, she increased fines for recusancy to £20 per month and made it treasonable to convert people to Catholicism.

When the Northern Earls revolted in 1569, many other northern Catholics did not join the rebellion, which suggests that many were satisfied with the settlement.

The Catholic challenge abroad

There was opposition to the religious settlement abroad, but circumstances delayed direct action until later in Elizabeth's reign.

France

Although the French King, Charles IX, (right) opposed the religious settlement, he was distracted by the **Wars of Religion** (a period of wars and unrest between Catholics and Protestants in France 1562–1598). Relations between France and England were largely peaceful after 1564.

Spain

Spain also opposed the settlement, but it was pre-occupied with a revolt in the Netherlands in the 1560s (see **pages 36-37**) and wanted to maintain friendly relations with England to avoid a war on two fronts. However, by the 1580s, tensions between Spain and England had worsened, partly due to religious factors (see **page 33**).

The Papacy

The **Papacy** (the power of the Pope) opposed the religious settlement, but it didn't have the military strength to invade without support from France or Spain. Instead, the Pope, Pius V, told English Catholics not to attended church services in 1566, and he held out hope that Elizabeth's modest settlement might return to Catholicism in time.

By 1570, the Papacy had **excommunicated** Elizabeth (expelled her from the Catholic Church). Even though the Papacy didn't declare war on England, it was still dangerous because it encouraged and legitimised Catholic plots to depose Elizabeth (see **pages 29-31**).

Change   Elizabeth's attitude

Elizabeth responded to her excommunication with the **Treason Act**, 1571. This made denying her authority punishable by death and forbade anyone from bringing the **Papal bull** (an official document from the Pope) of excommunication into the country.

From 1574, the Papacy also began smuggling seminary priests (Roman Catholic priests who had been trained in Europe) into England to perform Catholic services and to train new priests.

Elizabeth responded with the **Act Against Jesuits and Seminary Priests** (1584) which decreed that Catholic priests in England either had to swear allegiance to Elizabeth or leave the country within 40 days. If they failed to comply, they could be charged with treason.

Edmund Campion, a seminary priest, preached privately to powerful families in Lancashire and then London. He was hanged in 1581 for treason. During this period, around a hundred other seminary priests were executed.

MARY'S CLAIM TO THE ENGLISH THRONE

Mary, Queen of Scots was the granddaughter of Henry VIII's sister, Margaret. Her claim to the throne was strong, and she posed a real threat to Elizabeth.

The threat of Mary

Mary was married to the French King, Francis II, and they were both devout Catholics. Her link to France and her rule in Scotland meant that some Catholics at home and abroad thought she should sit on the English throne.

Mary's route to England

1542	Mary was born and became Queen of Scotland when she was 6 days old. Regents ruled on Mary's behalf.
1548	Mary was betrothed to the French Prince, Francis II. She travelled to France and spent the next 12 years at the French court.
1558	Mary and Francis married.
1560	Francis II died, and Mary returned to Scotland in 1561
1565	Mary married Henry Stuart (Lord Darnley).
1566	Mary gave birth to an heir, James Stuart.
1567	Lord Darnley was murdered, and many thought Mary was responsible. She quickly married the Earl of Bothwell.
1568	Resentment of Mary, linked to Darnley's murder, led to a Protestant rebellion which deposed her in favour of her son, James. Mary was imprisoned at Lochleven Castle but escaped on 2nd May and fled to England to seek Elizabeth's help in regaining the Scottish throne.

Mary, Queen of Scots

Mary and Elizabeth

In 1560, Elizabeth had secretly helped Protestant rebels in Scotland who resented the Catholic reign of Mary's mother, Mary of Guise, who was ruling Scotland as Queen Regent. With help and troops from Elizabeth, the rebels defeated Mary of Guise.

Following the English victory, Elizabeth signed the Treaty of Edinburgh (1560) which stated that Mary, Queen of Scots would renounce any claim to the English throne.

When Mary returned to Scotland in 1561, the country was effectively ruled by Protestant lords. Mary denied that she had agreed to the treaty and wanted Elizabeth to name her as heir to the English throne.

RELATIONS BETWEEN ELIZABETH AND MARY, 1568–9

When Mary arrived in England, Elizabeth wasn't sure what to do with her. Mary's Catholic faith, as well as being an **anointed monarch**, meant Elizabeth had to tread carefully.

The problem of Mary

If Elizabeth helped Mary regain her throne in Scotland, she would win support with Mary, but she would also betray the Scottish lords she had put into power. Restoring a Catholic monarch to Scotland could undermine Protestantism in England.

Elizabeth could hand Mary over to the Protestant lords in Scotland but removing an anointed monarch (a monarch appointed by God) risked upsetting other European rulers in France and Spain.

Elizabeth could allow Mary to leave England, but Mary could join forces with France with the potential for a French plot to replace Elizabeth with Catholic Mary.

Elizabeth could keep Mary in England but that could risk her becoming a Catholic figurehead. If English Catholics rebelled, Mary would be the obvious choice to rule.

Although Mary was a threat to Elizabeth's rule, deposing an anointed monarch was also very risky, and could destabilise Elizabeth's position. Instead, Elizabeth decided to imprison Mary and ordered an enquiry into Darnley's murder to determine whether Mary had been involved.

Casket Letters Affair

The case against Mary was heard at York between 1568–9. Letters between Mary and Bothwell (the 'Casket Letters') were presented by the Scottish lords to show Mary's involvement in Lord Darnley's murder. The letters appeared to show Mary's guilt, but Elizabeth was reluctant to hand Mary over to her enemies in Scotland, so Mary remained in captivity in England.

This had three benefits to Elizabeth:

- Elizabeth didn't want to be the first monarch to execute another monarch.
- Mary's allies in France couldn't use her execution as an excuse to invade England.
- By keeping her in England, Mary couldn't reclaim the Scottish throne, which would have angered Elizabeth's Protestant allies in Scotland.

But it had two major drawbacks:

- As long as Mary remained alive, she remained a threat. Her presence in England meant she would be the focus of continued plots against Elizabeth.
- Elizabeth's reluctance to execute Mary caused friction in government because it split the opinion of her Privy Councillors.

Mary as heir?

One potential solution would be to name Mary as successor to the throne. Since Elizabeth didn't have an heir, this would resolve concerns about the succession and encourage Mary's obedience. However, appointing a Catholic heir was unpopular, as it might lead to civil war after Elizabeth's death. Naming a Catholic heir also went against Elizabeth's own Protestant beliefs.

1. Describe **two** features of the threat Mary posed to Elizabeth in 1568.   [4]

Mary was a legitimate claimant to the throne as Elizabeth's cousin.[1] Since Elizabeth's own legitimacy was doubted, as many Catholics didn't consider her parents (Henry VIII and Anne Boleyn) legally married, this made Mary a real threat.[1]

As a Catholic, Mary could drum up support from powerful nobles who wanted to restore Catholicism in England.[1] Mary also had ties to France and Scotland, so an invasion from abroad with Mary as a figurehead was a very real threat.[1]

2. Explain why Elizabeth chose to keep Mary in captivity in 1568–69.

You **may** use the following in your answer:

- France
- the Scottish nobility

You **must** also use information of your own. [12]

Your answer may include:

France:

- *Mary was the widow of France's former king, Francis II. Executing Mary would have created a powerful enemy.*
- *Giving Mary the Scottish throne could reignite the Auld Alliance between Scotland and France.*
- *If Mary left England, she would be free to conspire with France to overthrow Elizabeth.*

The Scottish nobility:

- *Returning Mary to the throne in Scotland would anger Protestant nobles in Scotland.*
- *Delivering Mary to the Scottish nobility who wanted justice for her crimes could anger France.*

Captivity in England:

- *This avoided problems with Scotland and France, but meant Mary remained a figurehead for Catholic plots in England.*

Other information:

- *Elizabeth was cautious and indecisive. Keeping Mary captive was the least controversial option.*
- *Elizabeth could have named Mary as heir to the throne. This may have secured Mary's loyalty but would have angered Protestants in England and possibly led to civil war on Elizabeth's death.*
- *Elizabeth didn't want to execute a fellow monarch. Elizabeth was in a vulnerable position and did not want to set a precedence for executing monarchs.*

This question should be marked in accordance with the levels-based mark scheme on page 61.

Make sure your answer to this question is in paragraphs and full sentences. Bullet points have been used in this example answer to suggest some information you could include. To get top marks, you need to include information other than the bullet points in the question.

EXAMINATION PRACTICE

Instructions and information:
- This page follows the format of the examination.
- The total mark for this section of the paper is 32. The marks for each question are shown in brackets.
- You must answer part (a), (b) and one option from part (c).
- You should allow roughly 50 minutes to answer the questions below.
- Write your answers on a separate sheet of paper using black ink.

1. (a) Describe **two** features of early Elizabethan society.   [4]

    (b) Explain why some people felt Elizabeth shouldn't be queen when she came to the throne in 1558.

    You **may** use the following in your answer:
    - illegitimacy
    - her gender

    You **must** also use your own knowledge.   [12]

    (c) (i) "The threat from France was the most significant issue for Elizabeth on her accession to the throne."

    How far do you agree? Explain your answer.

    You **may** use the following in your answer:
    - religious divisions
    - financial issues

    You **must** also use your own knowledge.   [16]

    (ii) "Puritan resistance was the most significant challenge to the religious settlement of 1559."

    How far do you agree? Explain your answer.

    You **may** use the following in your answer:
    - the vestments controversy
    - seminary priests

    You **must** also use your own knowledge.   [16]

THE REVOLT OF THE NORTHERN EARLS, 1569–70

In November 1569, two northern Earls rebelled against Elizabeth. It was the most significant rebellion against the queen during her reign.

Aim of the revolt

The revolt was led by the Catholic Earls of Westmorland (Charles Neville) and Northumberland (Thomas Percy) as well as their wives. Neville's wife, Jane, was the sister of the Duke of Norfolk, Thomas Howard. The aim was for Mary, Queen of Scots to marry Norfolk, overthrow Elizabeth with an army and put Catholic Mary on the throne. They also wanted to replace southern privy counsellors with men who would be more favourable to the north.

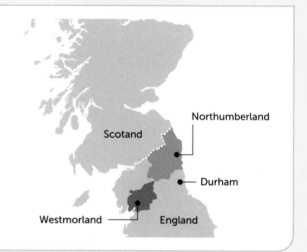

Reasons for the revolt

Power

During Elizabeth's reign, established families (many in the north, and Catholic) had lost power and influence to newer Protestant families in the south. Men like William Cecil and Robert Dudley were resented for their new-found influence at court. The northern earls were also angry that the **Council of the North**, which helped to govern the region, was controlled by southern Protestants.

Religion

Much of the north remained Catholic. Although Elizabeth's religious settlement appeased most people, the gradual replacement of clergy with Protestants and the appointment of James Pilkington as the Protestant Archbishop of Durham in 1561 angered many in the north.

Money

Both the Percys and the Nevilles had lost land to southern Protestants as Elizabeth redistributed money and influence amongst her new court. The queen had also claimed the rights to a valuable copper mine discovered on Percy's land in 1567.

Security

There was widespread worry about who would rule when Elizabeth died. In the north, there were concerns that a messy succession could lead to civil war and a future Protestant monarch. This could lead to further loss of power and influence in the north.

Key features of the revolt

It began as a plan to secure a marriage between the Duke of Norfolk and Mary, rather than a rebellion. However, sanctioning marriages and the issue of succession were both royal decisions, so this match went behind Elizabeth's back. Mary told sympathisers in Spain she intended to become queen "in three months", which suggests a deliberate intention to overthrow Elizabeth. Mary hoped that Spain would send support once the rebellion started.

Dudley (a close advisor of the queen) heard about the plot, and Norfolk was arrested. The northern earls responded to Norfolk's arrest by raising an army to march on Durham. The earls captured Durham and celebrated Catholic Mass in the cathedral. The Earl of Sussex raised an army of 10,000 men to confront the rebels. After the rebellion was defeated by Sussex's royal army near Tutbury, Westmorland fled to Scotland while Northumberland and 400 troops were executed by order of the queen.

Describe **two** features of the Revolt of the Northern Earls. [4]

The Revolt of the Northern Earls was led by Charles Neville and Thomas Percy.[1] They were angry because they had lost influence to newer Protestant members of the court, such as Dudley and William Cecil.[1]

Percy and Neville also wanted to restore Catholicism and a Catholic monarch to the throne following Elizabeth's religious settlement.[1] They intended to overthrow Elizabeth and put Catholic Mary, Queen of Scots on the throne.[1]

Elizabeth's religious settlement (see **pages 12-13**) was an attempt to appease both Protestants and Catholics in England by introducing religious changes which would be acceptable to both groups. Although the settlement was largely successful, some Catholics resented the changes and actively rebelled against them.

The significance of the revolt

The revolt gained little support from other northern Catholic nobles. This may have been because they were loyal to Elizabeth, or because they were fearful of the consequences if the revolt failed.

The rebellion created fear amongst Protestants in England. They worried that a successful Catholic rebellion could see a return of the persecution they had faced under Mary I.

Prior to the revolt, Elizabeth had tried to appease Catholics to maintain stability. However, after the revolt, Elizabeth's attitude changed:

Impact
The revolt showed the threat posed by English Catholics.

Elizabeth's response
Elizabeth strengthened laws to protect herself (for example the **Treason Act**, see **page 20**) and tightened measures against Catholicism (for example the **Act Against Jesuits and Seminary Priests**, see **page 20**).

Impact
The revolt showed that Catholic plots could get support from abroad.

Elizabeth's response
Elizabeth attempted to secure better relations with France, to ensure they did not conspire against her.

Impact
Mary, Queen of Scots showed she was disloyal and a direct threat to Elizabeth.

Elizabeth's response
Elizabeth refused to execute Mary, but she did keep her in prison.

Impact
Concerns about the loyalty of the northern earls, and the north in general, grew.

Elizabeth's response
Lord Huntingdon, Elizabeth's cousin, became leader of the **Council of the North**. Elizabeth wanted to appoint someone loyal who could prevent further uprisings.

Elizabeth's excommunication in 1570 intended to give Papal support to the rebellion, but the message didn't arrive in England until after the rebels had been defeated.

THE RIDOLFI, THROCKMORTON AND BABINGTON PLOTS

The Papal Bull of 1570 which excommunicated Elizabeth effectively gave Papal approval to plots to overthrow her.

The Ridolfi Plot (1571)

Roberto Ridolfi, an Italian banker and spy for the Pope, wanted to overthrow Elizabeth with a Spanish invasion and replace her with Mary, Queen of Scots.

The plotters wanted Mary to marry the Duke of Norfolk.

Ridolfi met the Pope, Philip II of Spain and the Duke of Alba in the Spanish Netherlands and took a letter from Norfolk declaring his Catholicism and support for Philip.

Cecil discovered the plot and used Norfolk's letter to prove his treason.

Elizabeth signed Norfolk's death sentence but refused to do the same for Mary, despite Parliament's wish that they should both be executed.

Significance

The Ridolfi plot showed the growing threat from Spain and led to further sanctions against Catholics in England. Laws passed in 1581 made it an offence to harbour Catholics or to convert people to Catholicism. They also increased the fines for recusancy, for attending Catholic Mass and made inciting rebellion punishable by prison or death. Elizabeth's refusal to execute Mary weakened her position with Parliament.

The Throckmorton Plot (1583)

Mary's cousin, the French Duke of Guise, wanted to invade England and put Mary on the throne.

Philip II promised Spanish financial support for the plot. The plot also had Papal approval.

Francis Throckmorton, an Englishman, acted as middleman to pass letters to Mary.

Walsingham (see next page) discovered these letters in Throckmorton's house and tortured him to confess, revealing the extent of the plot and a list of Catholic sympathisers in England.

Throckmorton was executed in May 1584.

Significance

The Throckmorton Plot showed there was a continued Catholic threat in England. It also showed the potential for France and Spain to conspire together against Elizabeth. Surveillance of Catholics increased, and many fled the country or were imprisoned. In 1584, the **Act Against Jesuits and Seminary Priests** (page 20) was introduced.

The Babington Plot (1586)

The Babington plot aimed to assassinate Elizabeth and put Mary put on the throne.

Anthony Babington, a Catholic, corresponded with Mary about the plot, but his letters were intercepted by Walsingham's spies and he and his co-conspirators were arrested, tortured and executed.

Significance

Unlike previous plots, Mary's involvement in the Babington plot led to her death. Elizabeth finally sanctioned Mary's execution in February 1587, (see **page 32**).

Elizabeth was popular, and the plots against her didn't have widespread support.

Difference   Elizabeth's patience ends

Mary had been implicated in plots before and Elizabeth had refused to execute her, so what changed? In 1585, Parliament passed the **Act for the Preservation of the Queen's Safety**. This stated that action against Mary should only happen if there was clear evidence, a commission established, and a trial held. By 1587, Walsingham's spies had secured this evidence, and Elizabeth was left with little choice but to sign Mary's death warrant.

Walsingham's Spies

Sir Francis Walsingham (right), Elizabeth's Secretary of State from 1573, was key to foiling the Babington and Throckmorton plots. Walsingham's network of spies and paid informants across England and Europe provided intelligence on potential plotters and his evidence directly led to the execution of Mary Queen of Scots in 1587.

Sir Francis Walsingham
(c1532–1590)

Ciphers

Eager to avoid messages being intercepted, Walsingham used elaborate codes (or ciphers) to disguise messages.

Agents provocateurs

Walsingham inserted his own agents into groups. These agents encouraged acts of rebellion, which could then be used to arrest a network of plotters.

Torture and the threat of execution

Walsingham secured information and turned potential plotters into informants.

Describe **two** features of the Throckmorton Plot. [4]

The Throckmorton Plot aimed to put Mary, Queen of Scots on the English throne following an invasion by her cousin, the French Duke of Guise.[1] *Francis Throckmorton acted as a middleman who passed letters onto Mary.*[1]

The plot was foiled when Walsingham discovered letters about the plot in Throckmorton's house.[1] *Walsingham tortured him to confess and reveal the full extent of the plot.*[1]

MARY, QUEEN OF SCOTS' EXECUTION

After almost 20 years of plotting against Elizabeth, Mary was sentenced to death.

Reasons for Mary's execution

By 1587, it was clear that Elizabeth's safety was at risk. Mary had been directly involved in several plots. As a legitimate claimant to the throne, Mary would continue to be a focus for potential Catholic plots, especially with Elizabeth excommunicated by the Pope in 1570. Rumours of invasion from Spain and evidence that Philip II had been directly involved in the plots made Mary's threat even more dangerous.

Mary was tried and convicted under the **Act for the Preservation of the Queen's Safety**, and Elizabeth signed her death warrant. Mary was beheaded on 8th February 1587.

Significance   Mary's execution

Mary's execution removed a legitimate successor. This meant Catholic plots no longer had a figurehead, but her execution re-established concerns about a potential civil war after Elizabeth's death. Elizabeth's decision to execute an anointed monarch angered Philip II, who was already planning to invade (**page 39**).

Explain why Elizabeth finally chose to have Mary executed in 1587.

You **may** use the following in your answer:

- the Babington Plot
- Sir Francis Walsingham

You **must** also use information of your own. [12]

Your answer may include:

The Babington Plot:

- *The Babington Plot aimed to assassinate Elizabeth and put Mary on the throne. Mary was directly involved in this plot, which showed that she was a serious threat to Elizabeth.*

Sir Francis Walsingham:

- *Walsingham's network of spies had become increasingly adept at uncovering plots.*
- *Walsingham secured Babington's letters which were clear evidence of Mary's involvement.*

Other information:

- *The Act for the Preservation of the Queen's Safety stated that action against Mary should only happen once evidence had been secured, a commission established, and a trial held. As this had been done, Elizabeth was left with little choice but to sign Mary's death sentence.*
- *Mary had been involved in numerous plots prior to the Babington plot. The Revolt of the Northern Earls, Ridolfi and Throckmorton plots had all aimed to put Mary on the throne.*
- *Previously, Elizabeth had been reluctant to execute Mary in case of a Spanish invasion, but by 1587, relations had worsened, so Elizabeth was less concerned about appeasing Spain.*

This question should be marked in accordance with the levels-based mark scheme on page 61.

Make sure your answer to this question is in paragraphs and full sentences. Bullet points have been used in this example answer to suggest some information you could include. To get top marks, you need to include information other than the bullet points in the question.

POLITICAL AND RELIGIOUS RIVALRY WITH SPAIN

Throughout Elizabeth's reign, relations between Spain and England became increasingly strained.

Political rivalry

England and Spain had been on good terms during Mary I's reign. Spain and France competed against each other, and they both wanted England as a potential ally. Spain needed England to protect its ships heading from Spain to the Spanish controlled Netherlands, whereas France, surrounded by Spanish territories, wanted a nearby ally.

However, from 1562, France was pre-occupied with civil war, and it no longer posed a threat to Spain, so the friendly relations between Spain and England ended.

During Elizabeth's reign, Spain was the most powerful country in the world. It had a large empire spanning Spain, the Netherlands and parts of Italy. Spain also had territories in the Americas, and in 1580, Philip II (right) also became king of Portugal. By the 1570s, Elizabeth had ambitions for an empire to rival Spain.

King Philip II of Spain (1527–1598)

Religious rivalry

Philip was a devout Catholic. This had meant peace with England under the Catholic Mary I, but once Protestant Elizabeth came to the throne and introduced her religious settlement, Spain was drawn into plots to replace Elizabeth with Mary, Queen of Scots.

Philip also presented a challenge to Protestantism that Elizabeth was increasingly pressured to respond to. Philip was attempting to wipe out Protestantism in the Netherlands, and Elizabeth felt as though she had a duty to support Dutch Protestants (see **page 36**). The Duke of Alba (a Spanish noble) also had 10,000 troops in the Netherlands, and Elizabeth felt threatened by a possible invasion.

Describe **two** features of the religious rivalry with Spain. [4]

Spain was a Catholic country, and opposed Elizabeth's religious settlement which introduced moderate Protestant reforms to England.[1] Spain responded to the settlement by supporting plots to overthrow Elizabeth and replace her with Mary, Queen of Scots.[1]

Philip was attempting to wipe out Protestantism in the Netherlands.[1] As a Protestant, Elizabeth felt that she had a duty to support Dutch Protestants against Spain.[1]

COMMERCIAL RIVALRY

During this period, countries were keen to display their power by expanding their territories, but war and exploration were expensive. When Elizabeth first came to the throne, England's debts meant that she couldn't compete with Spain.

Spain's commercial strength

Spain's colonisation of the **New World** (the Americas) during the 16th century had brought them huge wealth and access to markets and materials that England could only dream of. English merchants couldn't trade with Spanish colonies without a permit, so Spain controlled trade in the New World.

Spain also controlled the Netherlands, and in particular, the port of Antwerp. Antwerp was an important gateway to European trading markets. In 1568, Elizabeth seized Spanish ships loaded with gold bullion. In response, Phillip banned English trade with the Netherlands. This damaged the English economy and contributed to growing poverty (see **page 48**).

Change   Ambitions to rival Spain

At first, Elizabeth didn't have the money or resources to rival Spain's commercial strength. However, later in the Elizabethan era, English merchants began searching for new trading opportunities.

Sir Francis Drake

Sir Francis Drake was a merchant and sailor who was the second person to **circumnavigate** (sail all the way round) the globe in 1577–80, (see **page 52**). Drake was also a **privateer** (a privately funded sailor) who harassed Spanish ships and colonies. Although his actions brought treasure to his investors, including the Queen, they also contributed to worsening relations with Spain.

He was knighted by Elizabeth in 1581, aboard his only surviving ship from his circumnavigation, the *Golden Hind*.

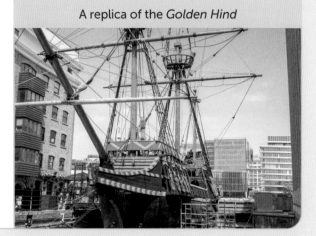
A replica of the *Golden Hind*

The significance of Drake's actions

Francis Drake's actions led to worsening relations with Spain:

- Spain felt threatened by the success of Drake's circumnavigation.
- Drake's knighthood, and the fact the queen supported his harassment of Spanish colonies and ships, was a direct insult to Philip.
- Drake pillaged Spanish treasure in 1572, which meant that Spain struggled to pay its troops in the Netherlands.
- Drake claimed land in North America and called it **New Albion**. This defied a Papal declaration that had given all land in the Americas to Spain and Portugal.

England's commercial expansion

Drake's actions encouraged other sailors who began looking for new trading opportunities.

Although English merchants weren't allowed to trade with Spanish colonies without a permit, many did so illegally, including Sir John Hawkins. Elizabeth secretly encouraged privateers who harassed and claimed Spanish ships for profit. Privateers also disrupted the flow of income from Spain's colonies, which caused financial headaches for Philip.

Describe **two** features of England's commercial rivalry with Spain. [4]

Francis Drake circumnavigated the world in 1577–80 and established New Albion in North America.[1] This angered Spain, because the Pope had stated that only Spain and Portugal could claim land in the Americas.[1]

English merchants wanted to trade with the rich Spanish colonies in the Americas but could not do so without a permit.[1] Merchants, such as Sir John Hawkins, took to capturing Spanish ships, pillaging colonies or trading illegally instead.[1]

ENGLISH INVOLVEMENT IN THE NETHERLANDS, 1585–88

Political, religious and economic tensions with Spain worsened during Elizabeth's reign, but the conflict over the Netherlands finally provided the spark for war.

Key features

Spain controlled territories in the Netherlands, but the growth of Protestantism in the Netherlands threatened Catholic Spain. Dutch Protestants began a rebellion in 1566, and the **Duke of Alba** (a Spanish noble) organised violent campaigns to try to reassert control. England was threatened and angered by the persecution of Protestants, particularly after the **Council of Troubles** (**Council of Blood**) in 1567, which saw thousands of Dutch Protestants arrested or executed.

Elizabeth's response

As well as wanting to support Protestantism abroad, Elizabeth also had commercial reasons for getting involved with the conflict. Spain controlled ports in the Netherlands, such as Antwerp, which were important trading routes into Europe. Spain had placed embargoes on these ports, and Elizabeth hoped that by supporting the Dutch, she could gain access to these trading routes.

Elizabeth also knew that if Spain was distracted by the rebellion in the Netherlands, a Spanish invasion of England would be less likely. Elizabeth was also keen to support the Dutch so that England had a Protestant ally nearby.

Wary of angering Catholics at home, Elizabeth initially used indirect methods to support the Dutch. She gave financial support to rebels involved in the Dutch Revolt, such as John Casimir. She harboured the Protestant **Sea Beggars** (Dutch nobles who opposed Spanish rule and harassed Spanish shipping in the Channel), and she encouraged English privateers, such as Francis Drake, to harass the Spanish at sea.

The port of Antwerp is attacked by the Spanish

Treaty of Nonsuch

By 1585, Elizabeth decided the Dutch rebels needed more help. In August, England signed the **Treaty of Nonsuch** with Protestant rebels in the Netherlands. The treaty promised direct support with an army of 7,400 under Robert Dudley, Earl of Leicester.

Despite signing the treaty, Elizabeth still wanted to negotiate with Philip. She didn't see the treaty as a declaration of war.

Although Dudley's campaign (1585–88) did not achieve its aims, it did secure the port of Ostend which was strategically important during the Spanish Armada (see page 40).

Relations between England and Spain

In 1585, relations between England and Spain were strained.

Political

The Treaty of Nonsuch and Elizabeth's direct commitment to troops in the Netherlands.

Commercial

England's desire to access Dutch ports.

England unlawfully trading with Spanish colonies in the New World.

The nuisance caused by English privateers raiding Spanish ships, and Elizabeth's knighthood of prominent privateer, Francis Drake.

Religious

France and Spain's commitment to tackling Protestantism, which was backed by the Pope.

Causation   Relations with Spain

By 1586, Philip was prepared to go to war with England, and he began planning to invade (**page 39**).

Explain why Elizabeth decided to involve England with the Dutch rebellion in the Netherlands.

You **may** use the following in your answer:

- Protestantism
- the Duke of Alba

You **must** also use information of your own.   [12]

Your answer may include:

Protestantism:

- *As a Protestant, Elizabeth wanted to support and defend Protestantism abroad.*
- *A Protestant ally in Europe could help England against any invasions from France or Spain.*
- *Elizabeth was angered and threatened by the treatment of Dutch rebels, particularly after the Council of Troubles.*

The Duke of Alba:

- *The Duke of Alba had an army of 10,000 men in the Netherlands, which could be used to invade England. Supporting the Protestant rebels would distract Spain from using this army to invade England.*

Other information:

- *The Spanish Netherlands, and in particular Antwerp, were the gateway for much of England's trade with Europe. The conflict in the Netherlands and trade embargoes threatened to hurt the English economy, so Elizabeth hoped involvement would allow her access to Antwerp.*

This question should be marked in accordance with the levels-based mark scheme on page 61.

Make sure your answer to this question is in paragraphs and full sentences. Bullet points have been used in this example answer to suggest some information you could include. To get top marks, you need to include information other than the bullet points in the question.

DRAKE AND THE RAID ON CADIZ

Although Elizabeth was still keen to negotiate, Philip viewed the Treaty of Nonsuch (1585) as a declaration of war. In January 1586 he started planning to invade England and began building a great invasion fleet, the Armada.

Drake's attack on Cadiz

In March 1587, Elizabeth sent Drake to spy on the Spanish fleet and to disrupt their preparations. Over the course of 3 days in April, Drake attacked the Spanish ships in the port of Cadiz, destroying 30 ships and claiming tonnes of provisions, such as wood used to make barrels.

After the raid, Drake sailed home along the coast of Portugal. He seized more ships and supplies destined for the Armada.

Drake also captured the *San Felipe*, a Spanish trading ship that was transporting gold, silk, and spices from the New World. This valuable cargo provided a financial boost to England.

The raid on Cadiz put preparations for the Armada back at least a year, allowing England more time to prepare. It was also very costly for Spain to replace the damaged ships and stolen goods.

The attack was called **'Singeing the King of Spain's beard'**.

REASONS FOR THE SPANISH ARMADA

The Spanish Armada launched in 1588, a year after Mary, Queen of Scots was executed. However the Armada was not a response to Mary's death; a fleet of this size required years of preparation and planning.

Long-term reasons

1

Spain wanted to remove a Protestant monarch in the name of Catholicism. This was supported by the Pope, who offered **absolution** (religious forgiveness) and reward to sailors in the Armada.

2

Spain was angered by England's involvement in the Netherlands and Drake's privateering.

3

England's ambitions to expand into new overseas territories threatened Spanish exploration.

4

Domestic plots to replace Elizabeth with Mary had all failed.

Short-term reasons

1

Philip saw The Treaty of Nonsuch (1585) as a declaration of war.

2

Spanish success in the Netherlands under the Duke of Parma gave Philip an opportunity to use Parma's troops to invade England.

3

In 1580 Philip became King of Portugal, so he had more ships and ports to launch an invasion from.

4

Elizabeth's initial reluctance to execute Mary made her appear cautious and weak, which encouraged Philip's plans for an invasion.

Philip's strategy

The Armada consisted of about 130 ships, 8,000 sailors and 18,000 soldiers. It was the largest fleet ever created, and Philip thought it was invincible. Under the command of the Duke of Medina-Sidonia, the fleet planned to sail to the English Channel, and meet with additional forces led by the Duke of Parma in the Netherlands. From there, the fleet would sail to Kent and invade England.

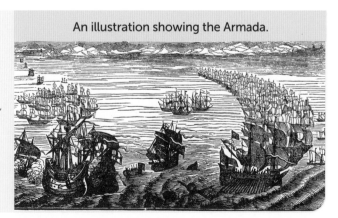

An illustration showing the Armada.

REASONS FOR THE ENGLISH VICTORY

The Armada seemed destined to succeed, but various factors led to its defeat.

Bad Spanish planning

The Duke of Medina-Sidonia planned to sail the Armada via the English Channel to collect the Duke of Parma's troops in the Netherlands. This required quick communication and for the troops to board the Armada swiftly. However, the Duke of Medina-Sidonia's ships were under constant harassment from the English navy and with no deep-water ports (such as Ostend) to anchor safely, the duke's army was late and slow in leaving on smaller ships to join the Armada.

Drake's raid on Cadiz

Drake's attack on Cadiz had two significant impacts:

- Drake had stolen barrel wood, which was used to store food and water, so the Spanish had to use inferior wood that couldn't preserve supplies for as long. As a result, Spanish food and water spoiled during the journey, which led to low morale amongst the crew.
- Drake's raid delayed the invasion by a year which gave the English navy more time to prepare. The English built more manoeuvrable **galleons** with longer-range cannons. This meant that English ships were quicker, and they could inflict damage on the Spanish fleet from a safe distance.

English seamanship and tactics

Although there were skirmishes off Plymouth (31st July) and the Isle of Wight (3–4th August), it was Drake's use of **fireships** (small ships that had been set alight) that sealed the Armada's fate. The fireships caused Spanish captains to panic, cut their anchors, break their defensive formation, and set adrift. The Spanish ships attempted to regroup at **Gravelines**, France but the English fleet attacked, and the Armada retreated towards Scotland. An English fleet followed them north to make sure they didn't double-back.

Bad luck and a lack of knowledge

Gale-force winds destroyed many Spanish ships as they tried to return to Spain around Scotland and Ireland. The Spanish sailors were unfamiliar with the dangerous coastline which caused several shipwrecks. Limited supplies meant that the crews suffered from starvation on the journey home.

Less than half the fleet returned to Spain, and thousands of men died during the failed invasion.

The return route of the remaining Armada

Britain

Route taken to invade England

France

Spain

THE CONSEQUENCES OF THE ENGLISH VICTORY

The English victory over the Armada helped strengthen Elizabeth's reign, Protestantism and English exploration.

Elizabeth's reign

Victory over the Armada boosted Elizabeth's position in England. She used propaganda, including a famous speech to troops at Tilbury, a commemorative medal, a new portrait, and a parade through London to reinforce her strength and authority as queen.

This portrait of Elizabeth was commissioned following the defeat of the Armada.

Religion

England's victory over Spain was interpreted by some as a sign that God favoured Protestantism.

The victory also reignited Dutch Protestant hopes that they could remove Spanish control in Dutch territories. This reinforced the Protestant Netherlands as a European ally for an otherwise isolated England.

English seafaring

England's overseas ambitions had increased during Elizabeth's reign, but they were no match for the established and wealthy Spanish empire. After the Armada's defeat, it was easier to see England as an emerging seafaring power, and overseas trade could be supported by a strong navy.

1. Describe **two** features of the English victory over the Armada. [4]

   English naval tactics were successful in defeating the Armada.[1] Drake's use of fireships caused the Armada to break their defensive formation and sail away.[1]

   The English navy had ships that were better suited to warfare.[1] English galleons had longer-range cannons which meant they could inflict damage on the Spanish fleet from a safer distance.[1]

2. "Drake's raid on Cadiz was the most significant factor in the defeat of the Armada in 1588."

How far do you agree? Explain your answer.

You **may** use the following in your answer:

- English ships and tactics
- the Duke of Parma's forces

You **must** also use information of your own. [16]

Your answer may include:

Agree:

Drake's raid on Cadiz:

- *Drake's raid on Cadiz damaged Spanish ships and delayed the Armada by around a year. This gave England more time to prepare and to build and equip ships.*
- *Drake's raid also stole valuable supplies such as barrel wood used to store food on Spanish ships. This led to a lack of provisions and poor morale amongst the crew.*

Disagree:

English ships and tactics:

- *England built new galleons which were quicker and more manoeuvrable. These ships were more effective for maritime warfare than the slower Spanish ships.*
- *The English ships had long-range cannons which meant they could attack the Spanish ships from a safer distance.*
- *The English navy harassed the Armada as they moved up the Channel and then scattered them with fireships.*

Duke of Parma's forces:

- *The Armada was very vulnerable to attack in the English Channel as it sailed to join forces with the Duke of Parma's forces in the Netherlands. The Spanish didn't have access to deep water ports, so the Duke of Parma's army was late and slow to join forces with the Armada.*

Other information:

- *The Armada faced bad weather when they attempted to return to Spain, which made the sailing conditions difficult.*
- *The Spanish captains struggled to safely navigate the dangerous route around Scotland and Ireland, and many ships were lost on the journey home.*

This question should be marked in accordance with the levels-based mark scheme on page 62.

To get top marks, you must refer to the question and make a judgement on the statement, having outlined the different sides of the argument.

Make sure your answer to this question is in paragraphs and full sentences. Bullet points have been used in this example answer to suggest some information you could include. To get top marks, you need to include information other than the bullet points in the question.

EXAMINATION PRACTICE

Instructions and information:

- This page follows the format of the examination.
- The total mark for this section of the paper is 32. The marks for each question are shown in brackets.
- You must answer part (a), (b) and one option from part (c).
- You should allow roughly 50 minutes to answer the questions below.
- Write your answers on a separate sheet of paper using black ink.

1. (a) Describe **two** features of Francis Walsingham's tactics to uncover plots. [4]

   (b) Explain why England and Spain finally went to war in 1588.

      You **may** use the following in your answer:
      - the Treaty of Nonsuch
      - Sir Francis Drake

      You **must** also use your own knowledge. [12]

   (c) (i) "Religion was the main motivation behind the revolt of the Northern Earls in 1569".

      How far do you agree? Explain your answer.

      You **may** use the following in your answer:
      - the Council of the North
      - the question of succession

      You **must** also use your own knowledge. [16]

      (ii) "Mary's involvement in the Babington plot was the most significant reason for her execution in 1587."

      How far do you agree? Explain your answer.

      You **may** use the following in your answer:
      - the Act for the Preservation of the Queen's Safety
      - Philip II

      You **must** also use your own knowledge. [16]

EDUCATION IN THE HOME, SCHOOLS AND UNIVERSITIES

The Elizabethan era saw new attitudes towards education, but change was slow.

Education in the home

Poorer families

Children from poor families lacked any formal education, instead they were taught simple work skills (boys) and household chores (girls). Children attended Sunday school from the age of six where they learnt to recite the Lord's Prayer and the ten Commandments.

Continuity — Attitudes to education

Access to education didn't change for the majority of the working-class population. Attendance at school was optional, and parents either couldn't afford to send their children to school or couldn't spare them. Working-class children needed to work to contribute to the household income.

Noble families

Boys and girls were educated separately by private tutors with an emphasis on courtly skills and subjects such as classical languages, philosophy and theology. The highly educated Elizabeth set an example for noble girls. Noble children also spent time at another noble household as part of their education, learning the skills and expectations of their social standing.

Education in school

Petty schools

Children up to the age of 10 from wealthier families attended petty schools. **Petty schools** were set up in a teacher's home to teach basic reading, writing and arithmetic, as well as studying the Christian faith. Discipline was strict but bright children could progress to grammar schools. The equivalent of petty schools for girls were **Dame schools**.

Grammar schools

Over 70 new **grammar schools** were established in 1560–1580. These schools were privately funded, non-church and taught well-off (or talented lower-class) boys, often from towns.

For sons of merchants, artisans or yeomen, some grammar schools taught subjects and skills more focused on their likely professions, although many learnt their craft through apprenticeships instead. Terms and teaching hours were long, and punishments included exclusion, expulsion, corporal punishment or being 'on report' (observed and reported on).

Education in universities

As trade and commerce increased, so did the wealth and ambition of middle- and upper-class families. This led to more students attending Oxford or Cambridge (the only two universities in England at the time). Lessons were conducted in Latin, and undergraduate students (from the age of 14) studied Greek, maths, philosophy, geometry or astronomy. Students might then continue their education and specialise in law, medicine or religion.

Elizabeth encouraged the expansion of university colleges. She founded Jesus College, Oxford, and hoped to help to educate a new generation of Protestant clergy.

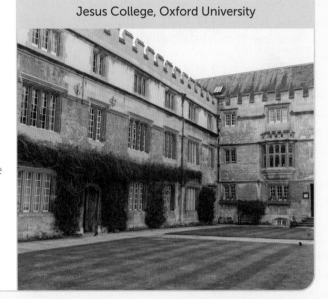
Jesus College, Oxford University

Change   Attitudes to education

Tudor social hierarchy meant early Elizabethan education was largely focused on practical skills and preparing children for their roles in society as less than 20% of the population were literate. Since most schools charged fees, education was largely reserved for the rich. However, attitudes towards education began to change slowly.

The introduction of the printing press increased the availability of books, and the gradual influence of **humanists** (a philosophical movement which believes humans have the right to shape their own lives) placed a greater importance on education. Protestantism's belief that the Bible should be in English and that reading the Bible was a way to connect with God also helped to increase literacy.

However, change was a gradual and limited, and literacy only improved amongst boys in this period.

SPORT, PASTIMES AND THE THEATRE

Leisure activities were influenced by social hierarchy.

Sports and pastimes

Nobility

Sports and pastimes amongst the rich were influenced by trends at court and what was popular with the queen. Hunting on horseback was common, as was hawking (hunting with birds of prey, such as falcons).

Noblemen were expected to know how to fence. Tennis and bowls were also popular.

These sports and pastimes all needed expensive equipment, so they were only played by the wealthy.

Ordinary people

Leisure time was limited by the pressures of work and religion, but festival days allowed working-class people to spend time on leisure activities.

Wrestling was popular amongst men of all classes, but only the working-class wrestled in public.

Working-class men enjoyed football. Unlike modern football, teams could have unlimited numbers, and villages often played each other on a pitch that could be any size.

All classes would gamble on cockfights (fights between chained cockerels with metal spurs on their feet) or bear baiting (a violent sport where dogs were set against a chained bear).

Playing sport was more acceptable for men than for women.

Literature, music and dancing

The popularity of literature, especially poetry and plays, increased during Elizabeth's reign. Common subjects included history and exploration.

Music was very popular in Elizabethan England, with people of all classes playing instruments. Lutes and harpsichords were popular with the nobility, whereas more affordable fiddles were played by the working classes. Music was studied at university, performed at public and private events, such as markets, plays and in churches, and was published as books of songs.

Both the upper and lower classes enjoyed dancing, which allowed men and women to socialise together. However, dancing was not an opportunity for different social classes to mix.

The theatre

The theatre grew in popularity during Elizabeth's reign. Elizabeth was eager to replace 'mystery' plays (plays that re-enacted Bible stories) that had been popular with Catholics, with secular (non-religious) plays. The growth of secular plays led to an increase in purpose-built theatres, such as the Red Lion Theatre and the Rose Theatre, where people of all classes could watch performances. Theatres were often open-air, and poorer people would stand in the pit (an area of the theatre in front of the stage) exposed to the elements whereas wealthier audience members would have sheltered seats around the edge of the theatre.

Comedies were especially popular, and the Queen and some other nobles sponsored groups of professional actors (or 'players'), such as the **Queen's Men** and **Leicester's Men**.

Only men were allowed to act in the theatre, so female roles were played by boys.

The inside of a replica Elizabethan theatre.

Describe **two** features of early Elizabethan leisure time. [4]

Sport was very popular amongst Elizabethans.[1] The rich took part in hunting and fencing while the poor enjoyed sports like football.[1]

Working-class Elizabethans didn't have much time to spend on leisure activities,[1] however, festival days were an opportunity for lower class Elizabethans to enjoy themselves.[1]

REASONS FOR THE INCREASE IN POVERTY

The main reason for the increase in poverty was population growth. The English population grew massively during the Early Elizabethan period.

Key features

Demand for food

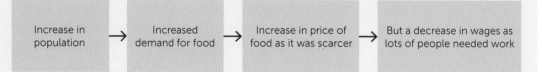

| Increase in population | → | Increased demand for food | → | Increase in price of food as it was scarcer | → | But a decrease in wages as lots of people needed work |

Poor harvests

In 1562, 1565, 1573 and 1586, **poor harvests** reduced the food supply, drove up prices and hurt those who farmed their own food (subsistence farmers).

Recessions

Conflict with Spain led to **embargoes** (bans on trade), which drove prices up and damaged jobs.

Competition for land

A larger population and more demand for food increased the demand for land. As a result, the price of land increased, and many couldn't afford the entry fees (money demanded up-front for land rental).

The wool trade

Demand for **wool** abroad meant more land was used to rear sheep rather than for producing food, which put more pressure on the price of food and land. Sheep farming also required fewer labourers, so there was less work available for farm workers.

Enclosure

Enclosure of land (dividing land into fields for animal or arable farming for profit) meant common land was fenced off, so this land was no longer available for people to grow food on. Larger farms led to more efficient farming methods, which meant there were fewer farming jobs.

Migration to urban areas

As enclosure, rent and poverty drove people off the land, populations increased in towns and cities. Larger urban populations needed more food, which further drove up prices as it cost more to transport food from rural areas.

Vagabondage and vagrancy

An increase in poverty meant more out-of-work people so **vagrancy** (homelessness) and **vagabondage** (travelling without a destination) became an issue in the early Elizabethan period.

Vagabonds travelled around looking for work, and often camped near towns. Areas where there was a large vagrant population often saw an increase in petty crime and theft. Vagrancy presented a challenge to the authorities, because vagrants moved around a lot, they were hard to control or punish.

Explain why poverty increased during the early Elizabethan period.

You **may** use the following in your answer:

- population growth
- changes to farming

You **must** also use your own knowledge. [12]

Your answer may include:

Population growth:

- *During Elizabeth's reign, the population in England increased significantly. This meant that there was more demand for food, which made food scarcer and drove prices up. Poorer members of the community struggled to feed their families.*

- *A larger population also meant that there was more competition for land. Land rents increased which meant that those with less money were priced out of the market and didn't have any land to grow their food on.*

Changes to farming:

- *There was a demand for wool abroad which meant that land that had been used for growing crops was used for sheep farming instead and crops that could be used to feed people were used to feed sheep instead. This contributed to less land for farming and a scarcity of food.*

- *In the past, poor people had used freely available common land to grow their crops. However, a rise in enclosure saw this common land fenced off, which meant poor people lost access to a place to grow crops.*

Other information:

- *A succession of poor harvests over the early Elizabethan period led to a lack of food.*

- *The war with Spain had led to a disruption in trade which drove up food prices.*

This question should be marked in accordance with the levels-based mark scheme on page 61.

Make sure your answer to this question is in paragraphs and full sentences. Bullet points have been used in this example answer to suggest some information you could include. To get top marks, you need to include information other than the bullet points in the question.

THE CHANGING ATTITUDES AND POLICIES TOWARDS THE POOR

Poverty had always existed in England, but the problem had traditionally been eased by monasteries.

Attitudes to the poor

In the early Tudor period, monasteries gave help and charity to those in poverty. However, after the dissolution of the monasteries during Henry VIII's reformation, this help vanished. Population growth meant less food and less land, so homelessness and poverty increased. Wealthier Elizabethans feared that poverty would lead to an increase in crime and disorder.

Elizabethans categorised poor people into three groups:

- The **helpless poor** were those who could not help being poor, either because they were infants, elderly, disabled or were ill (sometimes called the impotent poor).
- The **deserving poor** were those who wanted to work but couldn't find employment.
- The **undeserving** (or idle) **poor** were those who could work but chose not to.

Elizabethans believed that people deserved the right to improve themselves, but there was dislike and distrust of those who refused. Punishments were tough; vagrants could be imprisoned, suffer whipping, or even be hanged for begging.

Change   Attitudes to the poor

Elizabethan authorities recognised that many people were in poverty for legitimate reasons. This, as well as the increased threat of disorder, forced authorities to take measures to help the poor and introduce new legislation to reduce the problem.

The political response to increasing poverty

Existing measures

Charity was available for the poor. Wealthy people would donate money to charities or establish their own foundations to help the helpless and deserving poor.

Poor relief was paid for through a weekly **poor rate** (similar to a tax), which was collected by Justices of the Peace (JPs). This money was meant to be spent on helping the poor improve themselves, but it was not always collected.

New measures

Statute of Artificers (1563): This aimed to ensure the poor rate was paid by all and that all JPs would collect it. Imprisonment for non-payment was introduced and JPs could be fined £20 for non-collection.

Poor Relief Act (1576): To improve themselves and keep the poor in their local area, JPs had to provide the poor with wool and raw materials so they could make and sell items. Anyone who refused could be sent to new 'houses of correction'.

Punishments

Vagabonds Act (1572): Targeted at vagrancy, this outlined punishments for offenders, such as having a hole drilled in each ear (1st offence), imprisonment (2nd offence) or the death penalty (3rd offence).

It also attempted to tackle unemployment by creating a register of people who needed assistance in each local area. Local government was responsible for trying to find work for these people.

FACTORS PROMPTING EXPLORATION

English exploration in the 16th century lagged behind Spain and Portugal, who had successfully established colonies in the Americas and had been exploring Africa and Asia since the 1400s.

Factors that increased English exploration

Growth of trade

Conflict in the Netherlands (see **page 36**) meant English merchants needed to find new trading routes, and Spain's colonies in America showed how profitable exploration could be. This encouraged long-distance trade.

Private investment

English merchants couldn't lawfully trade with Spanish colonies, so many financed privateers to do so illegally. Privateers sought new territories to trade with (or steal from) for their investors.

The printing press

An increase in printing presses meant there were more books about the adventures and profit to be had from exploration. This inspired a new generation of explorers. There was also an increase in navigation books, including a book by Martin Cortés called *The Arte of Navigation* which was translated into English from Spanish. This explained techniques for sailing across open oceans.

New ship designs

England used new galleons against the Armada. They were much larger than earlier ships which meant they could sail for longer, carry more supplies and carry more cargo so journeys were now more profitable than ever before. Lowered bows and sterns made them more stable at sea, and long-range cannons meant they were better defended against Spanish ships.

New technology

Elizabethan sailors used **astrolabes** to help them navigate by measuring the angle between the horizon and the North Star. Advancements in mathematics also improved the accuracy of sailing. For example, Thomas Harriot devised a simpler way to calculate a ship's sailing direction.

Better maps

Gerardus Mercator's map used parallel lines of latitude and longitude, which helped to standardise maps and make them more accurate. These maps could be quickly duplicated through printing, which meant maps were more widely available, making it easier for sailors to plot voyages.

DRAKE'S CIRCUMNAVIGATION OF THE GLOBE

Drake's aims

Drake's voyage was privately commissioned by the Queen and members of the court. He was tasked with raiding Spanish colonies on the American Pacific coast and finding potential areas for English settlement. The voyage was done secretly because the rights to exploring the New World (America) had been given to Spain and Portugal by the Pope.

The voyage

Drake began his voyage in 1577 with five ships. After attacking colonies along South America, Drake kept going, travelling back to England with only one ship, the *Golden Hind*, and all 56 crew, in 1580.

The significance of the voyage

- It demonstrated England's strength as a global seafaring power.
- It returned a handsome profit for Drake and his investors, which encouraged other explorers.
- It provided maps and knowledge for areas they had explored.
- It inspired others, like Sir Humphrey Gilbert (see **page 53**), to establish English colonies in places such as New England.
- It enabled trade and exploration elsewhere, such as China, Africa and India.
- Tales of Drake's adventures inspired others to attempt overseas exploration.

Significance	Drake's knighthood

Elizabeth knighted Francis Drake on his return (below). This was a public insult to Philip II, who considered Drake a pirate. Drake's knighthood, and his raids on Spanish ships and colonies, pushed England and Spain closer to war.

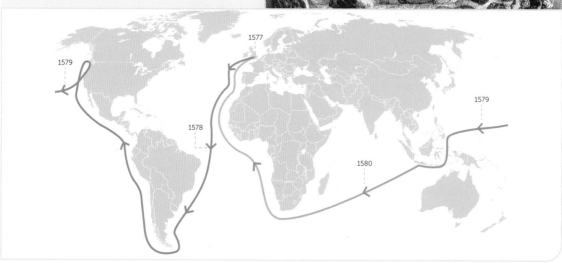

THE SIGNIFICANCE OF RALEIGH AND THE VIRGINIA COLONY

The success of Drake's circumnavigation encouraged attempts to establish English colonies in North America.

Benefits of establishing a colony

Establishing a colony in the Americas would allow England to access new resources (such as potatoes and tobacco), and to reduce dependence on European countries for goods. A colony in the New World would also give England a base to launch ships for further exploration and settlement, as well as challenging Spanish trade in the area.

Walter Raleigh (1552–1618)

English colonies in America

Colonising the New World was more difficult than anyone anticipated:

1578 Sir Humphrey Gilbert fails to establish a colony in North America and is bankrupted.

1583 Gilbert fails again on a voyage to establish a colony in North America and dies returning.

1584 Elizabeth issues one of her court favourites, Sir Walter Raleigh, with a grant to establish a colony but Raleigh did not lead the expedition. Instead, he organised, financed and promoted the mission and appointed a governor in his absence.

Raleigh sends an initial expedition to America to investigate ahead of establishing a colony. Reports are favourable and the explorers establish good relationships with the native population. These reports, and the profit made by Drake's voyage when he returned in 1580, encouraged investors.

1585 107 colonists, carefully chosen by Raleigh with the skills to build, feed and defend the new colony, depart for Roanoke, Virginia.

1586 Francis Drake visits the colony, and most of the settlers decide to return to England with him and abandon the colony after struggling with a lack of supplies and hostilities with American Indians.

1587 A second group of settlers reach Roanoke.

1588 Supplies are due to be delivered to the colony but are delayed because of the Armada.

1590 The delayed supply ships finally arrive, but the colony is found abandoned.

REASONS FOR THE FAILURE OF VIRGINIA

Raleigh promoted, planned, and secured funding for the new colony. However, Raleigh was also partly responsible for the colony's failures.

Food

The 1585 voyage left later than planned. By the time the colonists reached Virginia, it was too late to plant crops. Food packed on one of the ships, *The Tiger*, was damaged when the ship sprang a leak and much of the remaining food rotted in the humid conditions. Unable to plant their own crops, the colonists had to rely on the local population for food.

The American Indians

The fact-finding expedition of 1584 brought back two American Indians, Manteo and Wanchese, who were useful in establishing contact with the locals. However, the colonists were increasingly dependent on handouts and support from the local Algonquian population. Some members of the colony expected that the American Indians would work for them.

An attack by Chief Wingina in 1586 led to the abandonment of the first settlement. The second settlement may have been wiped out by a local tribe before 1590, however, the word 'Croatoan' was carved into a tree in the abandoned settlement, leading to speculation that the settlers had joined this tribe.

The colonists

The Virginia colony suffered some people issues.

The leader chosen for the first expedition, Richard Grenville, did not get on with the governor, Ralph Lane, which led to some poor decisions. The colonists were from different social backgrounds, and the upper classes weren't prepared to work. There weren't enough farmers, and the farmers in the group didn't want to farm for others. Merchants and soldiers were ill-equipped to farm the land, ill-disciplined or had unrealistic expectations about how quickly or easily they would profit from the expedition. Skilled artisans lacked materials, for example, there was no stone for the stonemasons.

Bad luck

Damage to the supplies on the initial voyage made the colonists reliant on local tribes from the very beginning. The second expedition in 1587 could not be resupplied due to the Armada.

1. Describe **two** features of the colonisation of Virginia. [4]

Unsuccessful attempts had been made to colonise Virginia before Raleigh.[1] Sir Humphrey Gilbert had failed twice in 1578 and 1583.[1]

Raleigh's attempts to colonise Virginia were also unsuccessful. [1] In 1586, most of the colonists decided to abandon the settlement and return to England when Francis Drake visited the colony.[1]

2. Explain why the settlement in Roanoke failed.

   You **may** use the following in your answer:

   - poor planning
   - the Spanish Armada

   You **must** also use information of your own. [12]

Your answer may include:

Poor planning:

- *The voyage set sail later than planned, which meant the colonists couldn't plant food for the first harvest.*
- *The men chosen for the first settlement had unrealistic expectations of how quickly the settlement would succeed.*
- *There were too few farmers and not enough materials for the skilled artisans.*

The Spanish Armada:

- *The settlement had been due to receive supplies in 1588, but the supplies were delayed because of the Armada. When the supply ship finally arrived in 1590, the colony had been abandoned.*

Other information:

- *One ship sprung a leak on the outward journey, ruining supplies intended for the first colony.*
- *Despite good relations initially, poor treatment of the American Indians and demands for food led to conflict in 1586 with Chief Wingina.*
- *The leader of the first colony, Richard Grenville, and the governor, Ralph Lane, did not get on. This led to some poor decisions.*
- *The farmers in the colony did not want to farm for the other members of the group.*

This question should be marked in accordance with the levels-based mark scheme on page 61.

Make sure your answer to this question is in paragraphs and full sentences. Bullet points have been used in this example answer to suggest some information you could include. To get top marks, you need to include information other than the bullet points in the question.

EXAMINATION PRACTICE

Instructions and information:

- This page follows the format of the examination.
- The total mark for this section of the paper is 32. The marks for each question are shown in brackets.
- You must answer part (a), (b) and one option from part (c).
- You should allow roughly 50 minutes to answer the questions below.
- Write your answers on a separate sheet of paper using black ink.

1. (a) Describe **two** features of early Elizabethan theatre. [4]

    (b) Explain why there was an increase in education during the early Elizabethan period.

    You **may** use the following in your answer:
    - an increase in trade
    - the printing presses

    You **must** also use your own knowledge. [12]

    (c) (i) "Drake's successful circumnavigation of the globe in 1577–80 was the most significant factor in the growth of exploration by England under Elizabeth."

    How far do you agree? Explain your answer.

    You **may** use the following in your answer:
    - developments in ship building
    - Drake's knighthood

    You **must** also use your own knowledge. [16]

    (ii) "The wool trade was the most significant cause of poverty in early Elizabethan England."

    How far do you agree? Explain your answer.

    You **may** use the following in your answer:
    - population growth
    - changes to farming methods

    You **must** also use your own knowledge. [16]

EXAMINATION PRACTICE ANSWERS

Key Topic 1

1. (a)   Your answer may include: [4]

In the country, status in society was determined by how much land someone owned, with nobles and the gentry at the top of the social hierarchy and vagrants at the bottom. In the towns, status in society was based on wealth and occupation, with merchants at the top of the hierarchy and unskilled labourers and the unemployed at the bottom.

(b)   Your answer may include: [12]

When Elizabeth came to the throne in 1558, some people thought that she shouldn't be queen. One of the most significant reasons was the question of her legitimacy. Some people doubted that Henry VIII had been legally married to Elizabeth's mother, Anne, when she was born. This was partly because Henry VIII had divorced his first wife without the approval of the Pope. Elizabeth's legitimacy was also questioned because Henry had declared her illegitimate for a period, although he later reversed his decision. Since being queen was a birthright, doubts about her legitimacy were taken very seriously.

Another reason why some people thought Elizabeth shouldn't be queen was her gender. Society considered women to be inferior to men, and many people thought that Elizabeth didn't have the strength or intelligence to rule a country because she was a woman. This belief was especially prevalent when Elizabeth came to the throne because her predecessor, Mary I, had had a chaotic reign with poor harvests and the violent persecution of Protestants. Many people feared that another female monarch would also have turbulent reign.

Other people did not support Elizabeth's reign because she was unmarried and seemed reluctant to choose a husband. If she died without an heir, there wouldn't be a clear successor, which could lead to fierce competition between those who thought they should rule, and a civil war could weaken England and make her vulnerable to attacks from abroad.

Finally, Elizabeth was only 25 when she became queen, and people were concerned about her youth and inexperience. This was even more significant because Elizabeth had been third in line for the throne, so no one expected her to rule. As a result, some people felt she wasn't properly trained or prepared for the difficulties and challenges of being a queen.

(c) (i)   Your answer may include: [16]

When Elizabeth first came to the throne, France was England's main threat from abroad, partly because Elizabeth had inherited a war with France from Mary I. One reason why Elizabeth was keen to end the war with France may have been because France was a Catholic country, and Elizabeth had reverted England back to Protestantism. Elizabeth may have feared that France could attempt to overthrow her and replace her with a Catholic ruler. This threat was even more dangerous since France had troops stationed in Scotland, and France and Scotland had an allegiance, known as the Auld Alliance, so an invasion from the north was a very real possibility. Furthermore, Mary, Queen of Scots, who was a legitimate claimant to the English throne, had married the King of France, and Elizabeth feared that a French invasion might aim to depose her, and put Mary on the throne. Therefore, at the start of Elizabeth's reign, France was a significant challenge the stability of Elizabeth's rule.

However, France was not the only challenge Elizabeth faced at the start of her reign. Elizabeth also faced financial issues as she had inherited approximately £300,000 of debt from previous monarchs. This was more than the crown earned annually. To make matters worse, Mary I had sold off crown lands which meant that Elizabeth's rental income was depleted, and Mary had also borrowed money with extremely high rates of interest. Furthermore, a steady debasement of English currency meant that foreign traders were reluctant to do business with English merchants which damaged the economy even further. Poor harvests meant that the English population were struggling, and it was impractical to raise taxes. Without money, Elizabeth would struggle to defend England if France invaded, so England's financial situation was also a challenge to Elizabeth's rule.

Another problem faced by Elizabeth was the issue of religious divisions in England. England had been Catholic under Mary I, and Mary had violently persecuted Protestants. Following years of religious upheaval, Elizabeth wanted to bring stability and peace to England by introducing her religious settlement. Although it was intended to be a moderate settlement that appeased both Catholics and Protestants, Elizabeth faced the possibility of backlash from powerful Catholic families, especially those in the north of England. Furthermore, the religious settlement potentially faced challenges abroad from Catholic powers such as Spain and the Papacy.

Elizabeth also faced challenges from those people who felt that she shouldn't rule England. Some people thought that Elizabeth wasn't the rightful queen because her father, Henry VIII, had declared her illegitimate. Although Henry reversed this decision, Elizabeth's position was still vulnerable at the start of her reign. In addition, as a female monarch, there were many who thought that she couldn't rule effectively. Society taught people that women were inferior to men, and that females weren't intelligent or strong enough to lead a country. This meant that people both at home and abroad thought that she was weak and vulnerable, and that Elizabeth could be easily overthrown.

In conclusion, although France was a real challenge to Elizabeth's rule, she was able to end the war quickly when she came to the throne. However, I believe that financial instability was the greatest challenge Elizabeth faced at the start of her reign. Without money, the crown couldn't defend England from invasion from France, Spain or the Papacy, which was a very real threat following Elizabeth's religious settlement.

(ii) Your answer may include: [16]   [16]

There was Puritan resistance to Elizabeth's religious settlement because many Puritans felt it did not go far enough. In addition, some Puritans opposed certain decrees made in the Acts of Uniformity and the Royal Injunctions. For example, Puritans opposed placing crucifixes in churches, as they felt crucifixes were a form of idolatry. In response, Puritan clergy demanded that they be removed, or they would resign. Elizabeth allowed Puritans to remove crucifixes because she didn't have enough clergy to replace those who would have resigned. Similarly, some Puritan clergy opposed wearing vestments, because they believed that everyone was equal in the eyes of God and that priests shouldn't wear anything that made them different to their congregation. Matthew Parker, the Archbishop of Canterbury, ordered clergy to attend an exhibit in London where he demonstrated the correct vestments and anyone who refused to wear them was stripped of the right to preach. This suggests that Puritans were vocal in their resistance to the religious settlement, and that Elizabeth had to make concessions to appease them

Elizabeth's religious settlement also faced resistance from Catholics in England. Only one bishop swore the Oath of Supremacy to Elizabeth, and those bishops who refused were replaced by Protestant bishops. However, replacing clergy who opposed the settlement was not sustainable. In 1566, the Papacy instructed Catholics to boycott church services in protest of the religious settlement. Although the Royal Injunctions decreed that there should be fines for non-attendance, Elizabeth often turned a blind eye, because she didn't want to provoke unrest and potentially make martyrs of those who didn't attend church. In addition, up to a third of the Catholic nobility were recusants, who practised their religion in secret. Although there was some passive opposition to the settlement, the Revolt of the Northern Earls was a significant act of Catholic resistance, as it attempted to overthrow Elizabeth. However, the northern earls who rebelled weren't solely objecting to the religious settlement, as they were also angry at a loss of power and influence during Elizabeth's reign.

The religious settlement also faced resistance from the Papacy. Although the Pope didn't have the military strength to launch an invasion on England, he was a vocal objector to the religious settlement. The Pope instructed English Catholics to boycott church services in 1566. In 1570, the Pope excommunicated Elizabeth, which expelled her from the Catholic Church. This was a threat to Elizabeth, as it effectively gave Papal approval to any Catholic plots against her. Elizabeth responded by introducing the Treason Act in 1571, which made denying her authority punishable by death. In 1574, the Papacy also began smuggling seminary priests into England to perform secret Catholic services and train new priests. Elizabeth responded with the Act Against Jesuits and Seminary Priests in 1584, which meant that Catholic priests had to swear allegiance to her or face a charge of treason.

Although there was Puritan resistance to the religious settlement, it was not significant and never led to attempts to overthrow Elizabeth. Furthermore, although there was Catholic resistance to the religious settlement, Elizabeth was able to avoid any significant threats by ignoring recusancy and non-attendance of church. Although the Revolt of the Northern Earls was a Catholic threat, the rebels' motives weren't entirely religious. Therefore, I believe that the Papal resistance to Elizabeth's religious settlement was the biggest challenge because Elizabeth felt threatened enough to introduce new laws to combat her excommunication and the increase in seminary priests entering England. These laws were punishable by death, which shows how significant the Papal threat was.

Key Topic 2

1. (a) Your answer may include: [4]

Walsingham's spy network was extensive and effective, with spies across England and Europe. Evidence that he secured led directly to the execution Mary, Queen of Scots for her part in the Babington Plot. Walsingham also used torture to get information. For example, he tortured Throckmorton to get a confession about his involvement in the Throckmorton plot and provide a list of other Catholic sympathisers.

(b) Your answer may include: [12]

Early in her reign, Elizabeth was covertly involved in the Dutch Protestant rebellions in the Spanish-controlled Netherlands. For example, she supported the Sea Beggars who harassed Spanish ships, and provided financial support to those involved in the Dutch Revolt, such as John Casimir. Spain had also placed embargoes on Dutch ports, including the important port of Antwerp. This damaged English trade, and meant Elizabeth was prepared to get involved with the Dutch rebellion to reopen trade in the region. Later in her reign, Elizabeth decided to support the Dutch more openly. She signed the treaty of Nonsuch in 1585 which promised direct military assistance. Philip II of Spain saw England's involvement in the Dutch Rebellion as a declaration of war.

England's overseas trade and exploration increased during Elizabeth's rule, and her decision to encourage Francis Drake and other privateers to harass, steal and trade illegally with Spanish colonies set England and Spain directly against each other. Drake's circumnavigation of the globe and his 'claiming' of New Albion in the Americas meant that Spain's control in the New World was threatened. This commercial rivalry contributed to growing tensions between the nations.

Philip II was Catholic, and he opposed Elizabeth's religious settlement. Philip's involvement in several plots to depose Elizabeth and replace her with a Catholic monarch, such as the Ridolfi Plot, further strained relations between Spain and England. After several domestic plots were foiled, Philip recognised he needed to declare war if he ever hoped to overthrow Elizabeth.

(c) (i) Your answer may include: [16]

The Northern Earls, Percy and Neville, were Catholic and they were opposed to Elizabeth's religious settlement. They also resented that a Protestant, James Pilkington, had been named Archbishop of Durham in 1561. The Earls aimed to overthrow Elizabeth and replace her with a Catholic queen, Mary Queen of Scots. Furthermore, when the Earls took Durham Cathedral in 1569, they celebrated Catholic mass. These motivations and aims suggest that religion was an important factor in the Revolt of the Northern Earls.

However, religion was not the only factor which led to the revolt. The Northern Earls came from established families who had long held influence under monarchs such as Mary. Elizabeth's decision to promote newer families, such as Dudley and Cecil, came at the expense of these northern families. The northern earls were particularly insulted that the Council of the North, which oversaw regional government, was controlled by southern Protestants. The earls hoped that the revolt would reinstate their influence, so a loss of power was also a motive for the rebellion.

Another factor which led to the revolt was a concern that the country would be thrown into a civil war if Elizabeth died without a successor. The rebellion started as a plot to marry Norfolk and Mary, Queen of Scots in a bid to resolve the succession issue. However, it was only when the match was discovered, and Norfolk was arrested that the Earls raised an army. This suggests that the rebellion was initially motivated by the issue of succession.

In summary, although religion was an important factor, I don't think it was the main motivation behind the revolt. This is supported by the fact that many Catholic nobles simply practised Catholicism in secret, and Elizabeth was prepared to overlook this for the sake of stability. Furthermore, the revolt gained little support from other Catholic nobles in the north. Although resolving the issue of succession was a motive, it's likely that putting Mary on the throne would have also given the rebels power and influence, which is something that they were desperate to regain. Therefore, I believe that regaining influence was the main motivation behind the revolt.

(ii) Your answer may include: [16]

The Babington plot aimed to overthrow Elizabeth and put Mary on the throne. Following the discovery of the plot, Mary was found to be directly involved and Elizabeth sanctioned her death warrant. Although Mary's involvement in this plot led to her execution, Mary had been involved with several other plots prior to the Babington Plot, so there were other reasons why Elizabeth decided to have her executed.

Following several domestic plots, Parliament passed the Act of Preservation for the Queen's Safety in 1585. This decreed that action against Mary should only happen if there was clear evidence, a commission and a trial held. Walsingham and his network of spies secured evidence of Mary's involvement, which resulted in a trial where she was found guilty and sentenced to death. This act provided legitimacy for Mary's execution, so it was a significant reason for her death.

Prior to the Babington Plot, Elizabeth had been reluctant to sentence Mary to death because she feared that executing an anointed monarch would anger foreign powers and lead to a declaration of war. However, by 1587 a war with Spain seemed increasingly likely, so Elizabeth was less concerned with angering Philip. The Ridolfi and Throckmorton plots had support from Spain, which highlighted that Mary was an important focus for foreign threats, especially Phillip II.

In conclusion, although the Babington Plot was a significant factor in Mary's execution, I believe that the Act of Preserving the Queen's Safety was the most significant factor, because it allowed Elizabeth to legitimately execute Mary without fear of repercussions.

Key Topic 3

1. (a) Your answer may include: [4]

The theatre became more popular with all classes during Elizabeth's reign. Lower-class people could watch plays from the uncovered pit area in front of the stage, whereas wealthier audience members could sit in the sheltered seats around the edge of the theatre.
During Elizabeth's reign there was an increase in secular (non-religious) plays, in particular comedies. Since women weren't allowed to act on stage, the female roles were played by boys.

(b) Your answer may include: [12]

One reason why there was an increase in education during the early Elizabethan period was due to a growth in trade and commerce. As trade and commerce grew, so did the demand for people who were literate and numerate so they could help with business. This meant that there was an expectation for the middle-classes to have a certain level of education. In addition, because of the expansion of commerce and trade, the middle-classes became more affluent. This meant that parents had more money to spend on education for their children.

Another reason why education started to expand during this period was an increase in the number of schools and colleges. Over 70 new grammar schools were established between 1560–1580 which meant that there were more school places available for children. In addition, Elizabeth founded colleges at universities, such as Jesus College at Oxford University, which she hoped would educate a new generation of Protestant clergy.

In addition, the introduction of the printing press meant that books were more widely available. This meant that schools had more access to printed resources, and that ideas and information were spread more widely.

The re-introduction of Protestantism also had an impact on the increase of education. Protestantism believed that the Bible should be in English, and that the Bible was a person's link to God. This led to an increase in people learning to read so that they could access the teachings of the Bible.

(c) (i) Your answer may include: [16]

Sir Francis Drake's circumnavigation of the globe between 1577–80 was a significant achievement which encouraged the growth of exploration. Since it was only the second successful circumnavigation, it proved that England was an important seafaring power. The voyage was very profitable for Drake and his investors, and Elizabeth publicly knighted Drake on his return. This showed that exploration could lead to wealth and recognition which inspired others. Drake's voyage also provided maps and knowledge of places that they had explored, which made it easier for others to explore overseas.

However, Drake's achievement was not the only factor in an increase in exploration during this time. Developments in naval techniques and mathematics made navigation far easier, for example astrolabes improved the accuracy of sailing. Developments in ship designs, such as galleons, also had a significant impact on the growth of exploration. Galleons were larger than previous ships and could carry more supplies and cargo over greater distances. Galleons were also more stable at sea and were equipped with long-range cannons which meant they were better defended against Spanish ships. This meant that voyages could be more profitable and safer for explorers.

Commercial reasons also played an important part in the increase in Elizabethan exploration. Conflict in the Netherlands led to trade embargoes, and restrictions on trading with Spanish colonies in the Americas meant English merchants and privateers needed to find new countries for trade. Wealthy patrons, such as the queen, would privately invest in privateers which meant that there were more opportunities for exploration and a greater potential for reward.

The introduction of the printing press helped to encourage the growth of exploration. Important books about sailing, such as the *The Arte of Navigation* by Martin Cortés, taught English sailors how to safely navigate across open oceans. In addition, the printing press meant that maps could be duplicated more easily. The availability of maps meant that sailors could plot their journeys more successfully.

In summary, although there were several factors which led to an increase in exploration, I agree that Drake's circumnavigation was the most important because the celebration of his achievement and the wealth and recognition it brought him inspired more Elizabethan explorers.

(ii) Your answer may include: [16]

The wool trade contributed to the growth in poverty in early Elizabethan England. Firstly, sheep needed more land to graze, so land that had previously been used to grow crops for food were instead used to rear sheep. The reduction in the amount of land contributed to a decrease in food production, which was worsened by some of the available crops being used to feed sheep instead of the local community. Furthermore, sheep farming required fewer labourers, which meant that there were less work available for farmers. Therefore, the wool trade did have an impact on the growth of poverty in early Elizabethan England.

However, the wool trade was not the only factor which affected poverty in this period. During the early Elizabethan era, the English population increased massively. This population increase led to a demand for food, which drove up prices. As well as contributing to a scarcity of food, an increase in the size of the population also led to more competition for land, and subsequently the price of land also rose, meaning that many couldn't afford the entry fees for land rental. A further issue caused by population growth was an increase in people looking for work. As a result, employers lowered the price of wages as labour became cheaper. Therefore, the growing population was a significant contributor to poverty in early Elizabethan England.

Another factor which led to poverty was a change in traditional farming methods. For example, common land that had been used by people to grow their own food was fenced off. This practice, called enclosure, meant that families no longer had land available on which to grow food. Another farming method which contributed to poverty was the growth of larger, more efficient farms. More efficient farming techniques meant that there was less work available for people which contributed to a growth in unemployment.

In conclusion, although the wool trade was a factor in the growth of poverty in early Elizabethan England, I believe an increase in the population was the most significant factor. A larger population impacted the availability of food and land, increased food prices and decreased employment opportunities, which all massively contributed to the increase in poverty at this time.

LEVELS-BASED MARK SCHEMES FOR EXTENDED RESPONSE QUESTIONS

Questions 1(b) and 1(c) require extended writing and use mark bands. Each answer will be assessed against the mark bands, and a mark is awarded based on the mark band it fits into.

The descriptors have been written in simple language to give an indication of the expectations of each mark band. See the Edexcel website for the official mark schemes used.

Question 1 (b)

Level 4 **(10–12 marks)**	• The answer gives an analytical explanation which is focused on the question. • The answer is well developed, coherent and logically structured. • The information given is accurate and relevant to the question. • The answer shows excellent knowledge and understanding of the period. • The answer includes information that goes beyond the stimulus points in the question.
Level 3 **(7–9 marks)**	• The answer shows some analysis which is generally focused on the question. • The answer is mostly coherent and logically structured. • Most of the information given is accurate and relevant to the question. • The answer shows good knowledge and understanding of the period.
Level 2 **(4–6 marks)**	• The answer shows limited analysis, and not all points are justified. • The answer shows some organisation, but the reasoning is not sustained. • Some accurate and relevant information is given. • The answer shows some knowledge and understanding of the period.
Level 1 **(1–3 marks)**	• A simple or general answer is given. • The answer lacks development or organisation. • The answer shows limited knowledge and understanding of the period.
0 marks	• No answer has been given or the answer given makes no relevant points.

Question 1 (c)

Level 4 (13–16 marks)	• The answer gives an explanation with analysis which is consistently focused on the question. • The answer shows a line of reasoning that is coherent, sustained and logically structured. • The answer includes accurate and relevant information that has been appropriately selected to answer the question directly. • The answer shows broad knowledge and clear understanding of the topic. • The answer reaches a well-supported and clear judgement. • The answer includes information that goes beyond what has been mentioned in the stimulus points.
Level 3 (9–12 marks)	• The answer gives an explanation with some analysis which is largely focused on the question. • The answer shows a line of reasoning that is generally sustained, but it may lack some clarity and organisation. • The answer includes accurate and relevant information, with good knowledge and understanding of the topic. • The answer gives an overall judgement with some justification, but some supporting evidence is only implied or not correctly used.
Level 2 (5–8 marks)	• The answer shows limited or unsupported analysis of the question. • There is limited development and organisation, and the reasoning is not sustained. • The answer includes some accurate and relevant information, that shows some knowledge of the topic. • The answer gives an overall judgement, but it is not fully justified, or the justification is insecure.
Level 1 (1–4 marks)	• A simple answer is given, which lacks development and organisation. • The answer shows limited knowledge and understanding of the topic. • The answer doesn't provide an overall judgement.
0 marks	• No answer has been given or the answer given makes no relevant points.

INDEX

EXAMINATION TIPS

With your examination practice, use a boundary approximation using the following table. These boundaries have been calculated as an average across all past History papers rather than an average of this paper. Be aware that the grade boundaries can vary quite a lot from year to year, so they should be used as a guide only.

Grade	9	8	7	6	5	4	3	2	1
Boundary	83%	75%	67%	58%	51%	42%	30%	19%	8%

1. Read the questions carefully. Don't give an answer to a question that you *think* is appearing (or wish was appearing!) rather than the actual question.

2. Make sure your handwriting is legible. The examiner can't award you marks if they can't read what you've written.

3. Make sure you revise the all the content well. You need to be prepared to answer a question on any topic, especially since the first two questions are compulsory.

4. Don't include any information that falls outside of the period. For example, don't mention Shakespeare when writing about Elizabethan theatre. He didn't start staging his plays until after 1588.

5. The examiner will be impressed if you can correctly use topic-specific vocabulary like 'recusancy', 'excommunicated', 'vestments', 'astrolabes' etc.

6. Manage your time well in the exam. Don't spend too long answering Q1(a), which is only worth 4 marks, and you don't need to write an introduction or a conclusion for Q1(b).

7. To get the best marks on Q1(b) and Q1(c) you need to go beyond the stimulus points provided in the question. You don't have to use the stimulus points if you're struggling to use them, but you need to discuss at least three different points in your answer.

8. It's worth jotting down a quick plan for Q1(c) to make sure your answer includes sufficient detail and is focused on the question.

9. Your answer to Q1(c) should make a judgement on the statement provided in the question. You need to use evidence throughout your answer to sustain and justify the judgement you reach.

10. In the longer written questions, use linking words and phrases to show you are developing your points or comparing information, for example, "as a consequence", "this shows that" and "on the other hand". This helps to give your answer structure, and makes it easier for the examiner to award you marks.

11. If you need extra paper, make sure you clearly signal that your answer is continued elsewhere. Remember that longer answers don't necessarily score more highly than shorter, more concise answers.

Good luck!

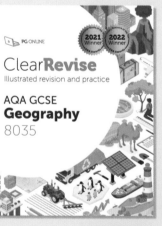

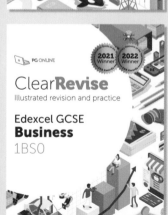